The Word Is Near You

Sermons For The Church

Don M. Aycock

CSS Publishing Company, Inc., Lima, Ohio

THE WORD IS NEAR YOU

Library of Congress Cataloging-in-Publication Data

Aycock, Don M.
    The Word is near you : sermons for the church / Don M. Aycock.
        p.   cm.
    Includes bibliographical references.
    ISBN 0-7880-1766-7 (alk. paper)
    1. Sermons, American. I. Title.
BV4253 .A93 2000
252'.6—dc21   00-034302
                                                                          CIP

For more information about CSS Publishing Company resources, visit our website at www.csspub.com.

ISBN 0-7880-1766-7   PRINTED IN U.S.A.

This book is dedicated to my best friend, who also happens to be my wife — Carla. Together we have lived in four states, parented twin sons (Ryan and Chris), pastored six churches, and made friends around the country. What a journey!

Together. What a sweet word. May it always be.

Dedicated to the first man to teach me the Word — Pastor Bob Bollich of Jennings, Louisiana.

Also dedicated to the First Baptist Church of Palatka, Florida. This is the greatest group of saints I know. Thanks, folks, for letting me be part of this pilgrimage.

Table Of Contents

The Attitude Of Gratitude

A Thanksgiving Sermon

Philippians 4:10-13

A group of tourists watched a grizzly bear catching salmon from a stream in one of our national parks. The bear would flounce around in the water until it managed to snag a pink trophy. It would then take a few bites out of it, toss it aside, and go after another fish. One of the tourists watching this show noticed this waste. Why didn't the bear simply eat all of its catch instead of wasting so many salmon?

As we gather here on this important day, we cannot but help feeling a bit like the grizzly in the park. We are surrounded by such bounty. We have an embarrassment of wealth. But like the hungry predator we seem to go from one bite to the next without being able fully to appreciate what we have. That is why Thanksgiving is such an important time. It offers the perfect opportunity to pause and consider just what it is that we do have. Paul's word for us is vital. Hear it again: "I know what it is to be in need, and I know what it is to have plenty. I have learned the secret of being content in any and every situation ..." (v. 12).

Someone has defined contentment as the power to get out of any situation all there is in it. And our spiritual ancestor Paul certainly knew how to do that. He wrote Philippians from a prison cell. Imagine that. From a dark, smelly hole in the wall comes the greatest demonstration of the attitude of gratitude. His chains actually gave Paul freedom to consider the most important things in life. He realized, as I hope we can, that much of what we think is necessary is only a luxury. For Paul, even captivity could not shake his courage and gratitude because freedom is not a matter of being without chains. It is a matter of living from one's spiritual center, despite any and all circumstances.

Thanksgiving Day gives us the opportunity, then, to get back to our spiritual roots, to recognize that life is so grand simply because God is good. If we forget this, then nothing else much matters. Abraham Lincoln recognized this fact. In an address in 1863 proclaiming a national fast day, Lincoln said: "We have been the recipients of the choicest bounties of Heaven. We have been preserved, these many years, in peace and prosperity. We have grown in numbers, wealth, and power as no other nation has ever grown. But we have forgotten God. We have forgotten the gracious hand which preserved us in peace, and multiplied and enriched and strengthened us; and we have vainly imagined, in the deceitfulness of our hearts, that all these blessings were produced by some superior wisdom and virtue of our own. Intoxicated with unbroken success, we have become too self-sufficient to feel the necessity of redeeming and preserving grace, too proud to pray to the God that made us!" If Lincoln believed this was true in 1863, what would he think today?

Paul's words are relentless: "I have learned the secret of being content in any and every situation...." He could get out of any situation all there was in it. When he was free to roam the ancient Mediterranean, he preached the good news about Christ. When he was shackled in some prison, he wrote the good news about Christ. You see, that news was the secret of Paul's contentment. Verse 13 reads, "I can do everything through him who gives me strength." Yes, there was the source of Paul's power, and for our attitude of appreciation for what we have.

Today is not a spiritual abacus on which we simply count our blessings. Doing that is certainly all right, but it is never enough to enumerate everything we have and then offer up a prayer of gratitude. Instead, today is a time to be aware of our greed, and to determine with Christ's help to keep it in check. Many of us remember the *Weekly Reader* we had in grade school. One lesson was on good grammar and it was showing children how not to run words together. The example was of the words, "Give me." The lesson pointed out that we should not say, "Gimme." It even had a picture of this character. He had eight arms all outstretched for something, and the words were coming out of his mouth, "Gimme, gimme, gimme." But for the grace of God we would all be that way, and sometimes we are anyway. But Thanksgiving Day helps us repent of the sin of "gimme" and instead to be changed by the secret Paul knew.

In Christ we are strong enough to get out of every situation all there is in it. On this day, then, we learn to share with Paul the attitude of gratitude.

God's Wake-up Call

An Advent Sermon

Romans 13:11-14; 1 Thessalonians 5:5-6

Everyone who has done much traveling knows what a wake-up call is. You spend the night in a hotel but need to be up at a certain hour. You call the switchboard and ask for the operator to call you the next morning at your needed hour. With those instructions given you can relax and enjoy a good night's rest.

The beginning of Advent is God's wake-up call to us. Notice how Paul puts it in verse 11: "The hour has come for you to wake up from your slumber." We don't want to be theological Rip van Winkles who sleep through the coming of God's Son. Consider Ephesians 5:14, and 1 Thessalonians 5:5-6.

What an unusual call this seems. But consider some of the implications of this mandate.

I. Wake Up To Theological Responsibilities

Faith is always lived in crisis times. That was true in Paul's day and in ours. The book of Romans addresses a church in theological conflict with its world. The Christ followers could not and did not fit into the theological molds of the first century. They were willing to give their lives if necessary to stand apart from their society.

Many people have observed that Christians today seem to stand for little that is different from society. If we profess to be Christian that profession may mean little because we are often just like everyone else. We may attend church regularly and even tithe our income. But if the change is not on the inside then the Advent/ Christmas gospel means little.

Wake up because salvation is nearer now than when we first believed. That is a theological responsibility because it touches our need for vigilance.

Mark Twain told about two paddlewheel ships that got into a race on the Mississippi River. On one, the crew broke up the cargo and put it into the boiler to make more steam so it could win. That ship won the race but arrived with no cargo. Let us be careful that we not end our race in life only to arrive with no cargo because we burned it all up on the journey.

II. Wake Up To Moral Responsibilities

Advent can be a crisis, so this is a good time to stake down the meaning of the season. You already know it is not about packages and trees and wonderful food. It is not even about family and home. Advent is the time of paying attention to our moral responsibilities. As Paul put it, "Let us put aside the deeds of darkness." We need not spend much time imagining lurid tales of violence. Those are in today's headlines. Instead, let us remember that Christ comes as light in the darkness. As vermin scatter at the coming of the light so do moral failures.

Keep a spiritual vigilance during this season. Also remember your moral responsibilities. What we do matters to God and to others. But forces are always at work to weaken our resolve. Early in the Christian era the Emperor Decius attacked Christianity.

Decius was a calculating man, and he decided upon a very astute course of action. He knew that it would be futile to set out simply to try to kill all the Christians. He would break them in their conscience. He demanded that they sacrifice to the Roman gods. But they were given many ways of dodging open sacrifice. This in itself tended to break down the moral fiber of the faith because it made many Christians parties to deception.[1]

III. Wake Up To Relational Responsibilities

The first half of verse 13 seems to describe some office Christmas parties: "Let us behave decently, as in the daytime, not in orgies and drunkenness, not in sexual immorality and debauchery." The second half seems to describe some church business meetings: "Not in dissension and jealousy."

These are relational matters. The coming of Christ affects how we treat each other. We relate as whole persons to whole persons, not as objects to objects.

Verse 14 tells us to take sin out of our will — don't plan for it; don't give it a welcome; offer it no opportunity; kick it off your doorstep and then it won't be in your house! God is giving the world a wake up call. His Son is coming. The light is dawning. Let us make no room for evil. Wake up!

---

1. Pope A. Duncan, *The Pilgrimage of Christianity* (Nashville: Broadman Press, 1965), p. 16.

The Mystery Of Christmas

A Christmas Sermon

Colossians 2:1-4

"... in order that they may know the mystery of God, namely, Christ...." What a strange thing for Paul to say! Wasn't he supposed to be making the intention of God absolutely clear? And here he is talking about the "mystery of God." At least he tells us what he means by this puzzle. Paul says the mystery of God is Christ. The more I think about this term the more convinced I am that Paul was precisely on target. Jesus really was the mystery of God. What better time than at Christmas to explore that mystery? Let us consider what the Bible means by this.

I. Jesus Was The Child Few People Expected

Oh, a few people had been looking forward to the coming of the Christ. Simeon, for example, in Luke 2, had been waiting for what he called the "consolation of Israel." He and a handful of others kept their ears and eyes open for a sign of what God was up to. But most people had grown weary of watching. Century after century had dragged on at a snail's pace. The Jews remembered the prophecies of Isaiah and others, that some day the anointed one of God would come to redeem the people. But so much time had passed and nothing had happened. Nothing! The time of Christ's birth slipped up on most of the people. They were not bad, or immoral, or irreligious. They simply did not know exactly what to look for, so they were taken by surprise.

So much was happening in the world into which Jesus was born. Caesar and Pompey had been struggling for control of Rome. Caesar was finally murdered in a conspiracy. Herod was appointed king of Judaea, which was soon annexed by Rome. Mark Antony and Cleopatra were defeated by Octavian in Egypt, and Egypt became a Roman province. Rome marched relentlessly through the known world, gobbling up country after country like they were

15

Christmas M & M's. Who could have blamed most people for not expecting a special birth in sleepy little Bethlehem?

The scene of what should have been a joyous celebration became a caricature, a cartoon of what it should have been. There is mystery in the Christmas story in the Bible, but also humor. Think of it. The harried innkeeper exhausted by his work, the shepherds scared out of their wits by the presence of angels, the wise men who hopped on express camels to follow the star — this is humorous in a deep and important sense. Bethlehem, which should have unfurled banners and played trumpets, slept through the second greatest event in history!

In the twelfth century in London, England, there was a priory, a place for monks called Saint Mary's of Bethlehem. The monks took in people with mental troubles and cared for them as best they could. The people around there began to talk about the place as a haven for lunatics. As they pronounced the name "Bethlehem" they slurred and shortened it so that it became "Bedlem." We use that word *bedlam* today to signify any place of noisy confusion. From Bethlehem to bedlam. What a strange transformation. But it is like what happened twenty centuries ago. The Christ who had been promised was born at Bethlehem. But so few were expecting the event. The quiet joy of that place has become the noisy confusion — the bedlam — of our trying to appreciate it. If you don't believe me, just visit a shopping mall tomorrow.

Christmas is mysterious because it tells us about a child nobody expected. It is also mysterious because it tells us that ...

II. Jesus Grew To Be The Man No One Could Control

John's Gospel tells us an intriguing story about Jesus, after he had grown up, being at a wedding feast. The host ran out of wine and Jesus' mother tried to get Jesus to do something about it. His answer to her startles us. He said, "Dear woman, why do you involve me? My time has not yet come." This seeming rebuke set the tone for much of what happened in Jesus' life from then on. What he was saying to his beloved mother was simply this: "You must not try to pull me from my course, or involve me in matters that do not concern me. I have an appointed destiny, and nothing will detour me from it."

People were always trying to control him, to squeeze him into their molds. The Pharisees wanted to make Jesus a keeper of their law. When he pointed to a higher Law, they were furious. The Romans wanted to make Jesus just a miracle worker, a circus performer. Luke tells us that when Jesus was arrested and brought before Herod, Herod was delighted. He had heard about Jesus and hoped to see him do a miracle. "Here, boy, jump through the hoop. Entertain me." That's all Herod wanted. Just a good show, a miracle, an afternoon at the circus. People are still trying to control Jesus in that way. They say, "Folks, it's in the Bible! Just name it and claim it. God wants you to be rich. He has to do it!"

The Pharisees wanted him to be a good Pharisee, and the Romans wanted him to be a good Roman citizen, and the Baptists today want Jesus to be a good Baptist. And he will be none of those things! Jesus is the Son of God who came unexpectedly as a baby in Bethlehem, who grew to be a man whom nobody could control and make in their own image. He paid the price for his refusal to knuckle under, but he kept his integrity. He seemed to be a loser, but he won!

Phillips Brooks is known to us as the composer of the Christmas hymn, "O Little Town Of Bethlehem." But he also wrote a description of Jesus which is widely known. Perhaps you have heard this:

Here is a man who was born in a lowly manger, the child of a peasant woman.
He grew up in an obscure village.
He worked in a carpenter shop until he was thirty, and then for three years he was an itinerant preacher.
He never wrote a book. He never held an office. He never went to college.
He never owned a house. He never had a family. He never traveled two hundred miles from the place where he was born.
He never did one of the things that usually accompany greatness.

He had no credentials but himself.

He had nothing to do with this world except the power of his divine manhood.

While still a young man, the tide of popular opinion turned against him. His friends ran away. One of them denied him.

He was turned over to his enemies. He went through a mockery of a trial.

He was nailed upon a cross between two thieves.

His executioners gambled for the only piece of property he had on earth while he was dying — his coat.

When he was dead, he was taken down and laid in a borrowed tomb through the pity of a friend.

Nineteen wide centuries have come and gone.

Today he is the center-piece of the human race and the leader of the column of progress.

I am within the mark when I say that all the armies that ever marched, and all the navies that were ever built, and all the parliaments that ever sat, and all the kings that ever reigned, put together, have not affected the life of man upon this earth as powerfully as has that one solitary life.

Jesus was a man nobody could control! He set his own course, and because he was true to himself, he has forever changed the human race. That is one of the mysterious lessons this Christmas season teaches us.

Christmas is mysterious because it tells us that ...

III. Jesus Was A King Nobody Wanted

His enemies laughed themselves purple. "Are you a king?" they mockingly asked. During the last two days of Jesus' life the people turned viciously on him. They hauled him before the authorities. Pilate asked him, "Are you the king of the Jews?" At the crucifixion a sign was placed on his cross, "This is the King of the Jews."

But what sort of king was Jesus? One like the mighty Caesar, whose bones were already bleaching in his tomb, one who caused untold hardship and bloodshed, one who sent army after army into battle for the sake of his own ego? Or a king like Herod wanted to be? Herod was so paranoid he had many of his own sons slaughtered to prevent them from trying to take his throne. There was a proverb whispered in Palestine during Herod's life: "It's better to be his swine than his son." The swine were safer!

Jesus would be a king, all right, but not the kind of king the people wanted. But the nativity should have clued them in on what he would be. He did not arrive in this world on golden clouds, announced to all the world by choirs of angels. He slipped quietly into a manger in Bethlehem encircled by only a few. The angels were singing, all right, but only a handful heard.

Jesus did not live as one of the mighty of the earth. He had no drafted army, but only chosen disciples; no throne, but only the highways and hedges of his world; no enormous treasury, but only a small bag of money for the necessities; no slave bands to serve his every whim, but only throngs whom he himself served.

At the very end he rode into Jerusalem, not as a mighty conquering king amidst the mighty armies, but on a lowly donkey with his little band of disciples following behind. After his arrest the soldiers put a purple robe on him and pushed a crown of thorns upon his temples — the only symbols of royalty he ever had.

Jesus was a king — a king unlike any who went before or came afterward. He was a king nobody wanted, because they just could not see what he was up to.

But he is king even now, in your life and mine. He is, isn't he?

Jesus came as a child nobody expected. He grew to be a man nobody could control. He lived as a king nobody wanted. But it is no matter. Jesus is Lord. Our only question is whether or not we will honor him.

At Christmas Time, Don't Miss Christmas!

A Christmas Sermon

Romans 15:4-13

A man who lives in Hollywood tells this to friends who come to visit: "When you are in Hollywood, don't miss Hollywood." He reminds his guests that his town is much more than a movie set. They won't see stars giving autographs or movie crews with cameras whirring.

In a similar way the Scriptures seem to say to us, "At Christmas, don't miss Christmas." It is easy to miss, isn't it? We can get so busy that the season passes over us like a plane at night, heard but not really seen. And what, during this season, do we need not to miss?

I. Don't Miss The Need To Keep Hope Alive

This is a season of hope and Advent is a message of the Church, Santa Claus notwithstanding. The merchants have practically stolen this season by their message of "Buy, buy, buy!" Even so, this season is about God who sent his Son into this world so that the world through him might be saved. Another word for this reality is hope.

A cave-in at a gold mine in Jackson, California, several years ago trapped 47 miners. They were surrounded by walls and ceiling and floor that was worth millions of dollars. But every man among them would gladly have traded every penny for another hour's worth of air. Possessions pale when life is stripped down to its bare essentials — the fragile dividing line between life and death. That fragile dividing line exists in our spiritual lives, too. Hope nourishes spiritual life to keep it healthy and vibrant.

We naturally think of this as a season of receiving, so think of what you can receive from God. One of his gifts is salvation from your sins. Another is a sense of belonging and purpose in life. A

21

third gift is work to do in his kingdom. All of this is part of the hope that is ours from our relationship with Christ.

II. Don't Miss The Need To Keep Fellowship Wide

"Accept one another," said Paul. But this is more than just "good buddy" feelings. Paul added the specification, "just as Christ accepted you." Paul is an archer here, pulling back in order to launch ahead. Verse 4 reminds us that the things written in the past are to teach us to have hope and to keep the ranks of fellowship wide. Although there is much sentimental nonsense floating around, one thing is positive — the emphasis on giving each other a break. This is more than custom. It is a biblical command — "Accept one another."

Leo Tolstoy, the great novelist of a previous generation, told of the time his native Russia experienced a great famine. A beggar stopped Tolstoy on the street and asked for a handout. Tolstoy said, "Don't be angry with me brother. I have nothing to give." The beggar smiled and said, "You called me 'brother.' That is better than money."

During the early part of this century Baptists divided into more groups than one could name. There were the Northern Baptist Convention and the Southern Baptist Convention; there were the American Baptist Association, the Duck River Association, and the Kindred Associations. There were General Six-Principle Baptists, Free Will Baptists, Separate Baptists, Regular Baptists, the Primitive Baptists, and one group I really like, the Two-Seed-in-the-Spirit Predestinarian Baptists.

The Church of God split off into a branch calling itself The True Church of God and then another calling itself The Only True Church of God. But what is the biblical principle here? "Accept one another then, just as Christ accepted you...."

Someone has likened Christian fellowship to a meeting of porcupines on a cold winter's night. The rodents come out of the cold and huddle together for warmth. But then their needles begin to jab each other so they go off alone. But then the cold drives them back together to huddle for protection. Then the spines jab each other. Then the cycle is repeated.

Many people this time of year are already tired, broke, preoccupied, and cranky. Contrast this with the fact that Jesus came as the Prince of Peace. Why not accept some of his peace in your life during this season?

III. Don't Miss The Need To Give God Praise

We also think of this season as a time of giving. What can you give this year that will express your faith and obedience? What about giving your life to Christ? We can also give gifts to the church to be used to spread the message about Christ and his love.

Perhaps the finest thing to give is praise to God. Paul breaks out into song in verses 9-13. Isn't that really the mood of Advent? The song is a series of Old Testament quotations that praise God for his including the Gentiles in his game plan. This calls for praise! It needs songs!

A *B.C.* cartoon shows the gang gathered around a piano. Refrains of some old favorites linger in the air: "Rudolph The Red-Nosed Reindeer," " 'Tis The Season To Be Jolly," "Jingle Bells," "I'm Dreaming Of A White Christmas." A loud shout comes from Gronk: "You dummies forgot Birthday Boy!"

It is a season for praise, isn't it? The next time you enter a store listen for what is on the store's channel. You will hear strains of "Rudolph" but you will also hear, "O Come, All Ye Faithful"..."O come let us adore him, Christ the Lord." "I'm Dreaming Of A White Christmas" will play back-to-back with "Away in a manger, no crib for a bed, the little Lord Jesus lay down his sweet head." It is an interesting mix of the secular and sacred.

At Christmas, don't miss Christmas. There is meaning behind the madness.

Affirmations For A New Year

A New Year Sermon

Isaiah 55:6

January is named after the Roman god, Janus. He is pictured as having faces on both sides of his head so he could see both behind and ahead. Let us look both ways. These reflections are things I have learned along the way. If any of them help you in your journey then I will have accomplished my purpose today.

1. Today Is A Precious Gift From God

How many of us have made New Year's Resolutions? A resolution is a promise we make to ourselves that we will do things differently in the future. I live with the expectation of a future. But today is all I really have.

The Bible is a picture of our possible life with God. That picture shows us many aspects of that life. One of the most significant is the importance of today. Isaiah 55:6: "Seek the Lord while he may be found; call on him while he is near."

Or consider Hebrews 3:14-15: "We have come to share in Christ if we hold firmly till the end the confidence we had at first. As has been said, 'Today, if you hear his voice, do not harden your hearts as you did in the rebellion.' "

The ancient Greeks knew this. They pictured time as a man with long hair in the front of his head and bald on the back of his head. The image is that you must catch time coming toward you. Once he passes, there is nothing to grab onto. What comes to us now is today.

2. Respect The Past But Don't Live There

Some of us might be planning to go to a party. But let me ask you to avoid one kind. Do not plan to be the guest of honor at a "pity party." Avoid the temptation to wallow in past failures at the expense of the present. All of us have troubles, problems, and

25

regrets about things we have done in the past. But be careful not to let the past bind and blind you.

If you've have some tough blows in the past, deal with them. Forgive people who have hurt you and make up your mind to live in the light and the love of God. The apostle Paul put it this way: "One thing I do: Forgetting what is behind and straining toward what is ahead, I press on toward the goal to win the prize for which God has called me heavenward in Christ Jesus" (Philippians 3:13b).

3. If It's Right, Do It; If It's Wrong, Avoid It

There seems to be an awful lot of mush being passed off as ethics these days. Thinking seems to be turned on its head. Morality is called "unnecessary restrictions." Immorality is called "my right to choose." Not only our children, but even adults are affected by this sort of thinking. As we look at entering a new year, I urge you to live simply and straightforwardly. If it's right, do it. If it's wrong, avoid it. Consider Psalm 1.

Character is formed by many small decisions. If I choose today to do something I know is wrong, then I will have an easier time choosing wrong the next time, and the next, and the next. On the other hand, if I choose to do what I know is right, even at the risk of embarrassment, then the next decision for right will be easier, and the next, and the next.

4. Remember That Everybody Carries a Heavy Load

I get the impression that many people imagine that there are "superhumans" out there — people who have no troubles, no pressures, no heartaches. There are no such people. Everyone is carrying a heavy load, so be kind. Job 5:6-7 puts it this way: "For hardship does not spring from the soil, nor does trouble sprout from the ground. Yet man is born to trouble as surely as sparks fly upward."

A few months ago I was in my yard when I saw a bee attack an aphid. I had never seen that happen so I knelt down and watched closely. The bee repeatedly stung the aphid. Then the bee did a strange thing. It took the aphid in its jaws and cut it in two. The head and the first two legs were separated from the rest of the body.

The bee then flew off with the body while the aphid's head and front legs were left to walk around aimlessly!

I know people who seem to live like that. Their heart has been cut out of them by some experience and they seem to wander aimlessly through life. One woman whose husband died said to me once, "I am a walking napkin ring because my life has a huge hole in it."

Life is hard. It really is. Tough. Painful. Unpredictable. No wonder our faith calls us to give each other a hand up once in a while. Paul says again in Galatians 6:9-10: "Let us not become weary in doing good, for at the proper time we will reap a harvest if we do not give up. Therefore, as we have opportunity, let us do good to all people, especially to those who belong to the family of believers."

5. The Only Things That Really Last Are Spiritual Realities

With one exception, everything we attain in this life passes away sooner or later. That one exception is the reality of the spirit. Spiritual realities last while everything else evaporates like dew in the morning sunshine.

Paul learned that truth. In Philippians 2:8-9 he wrote: "I consider everything a loss compared to the surpassing greatness of knowing Christ Jesus my Lord, for whose sake I have lost all things. I consider them rubbish, that I may gain Christ and be found in him, not having a righteousness of my own that comes from the law, but that which is through faith in Christ — the righteousness that comes from God and is by faith."

A contemporary of ours learned that. He is Air Force Captain Scott O'Grady. He was flying a mission over Bosnia and was shot down. He spent six days hiding before being rescued. We might expect that experience to have devastated him, but let me tell you the aftermath in O'Grady's own words: "While I didn't bring a new person into the world, I underwent a rebirth of my own. Those six days in Bosnia became a religious retreat for me, a total spiritual renewal. I'm not recommending near-death experience for its own sake. It's a ride I wouldn't care to take again. But I will say that my time in Bosnia was completely positive — nothing bad has come out of it. From the instant that my plane blew up around me, I opened my heart to God's love. That day, five miles up, with death at my front door, I found my key to life. It took a mighty big jolt to open my eyes, but it was worth it. I knew I'd never be lost again."[1]

6. God Really Does Love You

This is our theme song, our reason for being, and our central message. But sometimes we forget it. God really, really loves us.

My phone rang one morning. It was Barbara's family. She had been fighting cancer for years and was back in the hospital. The doctor said it looked bad. I went to the hospital and walked into the room, took one look at her, and knew the doctor was right. Barbara saw me and strained to speak. Although she had been a church member for years and had taught a class, she asked one question: "Does God *really* love me?" I gathered the family and we knelt by her bed, holding hands, and prayed. After a while Barbara said, "It is true, isn't it?" I wasn't surprised when the phone rang again late that night. She had just died. I thought, "Barbara, you know now, don't you?"

As Paul said in Philippians 1:21: "For to me, to live is Christ and to die is gain."

7. Look Forward In Faith

I said earlier to live for today because that's all we have. But our faith does help us look ahead. We won't know the details of what will happen, but we have read the last chapter of the book so we know the ending. We get clobbered along the way but that shouldn't stop us. Have you ever read about Paul's life in 2 Corinthians 4:8-10? He wrote, "We are hard pressed on every side, but not crushed; perplexed, but not in despair; persecuted, but not abandoned; struck down, but not destroyed."

What a horrible thing to live without faith or hope. While a company of people were having dinner together, one man in the party, who had spent many summers in Maine, fascinated his companions by telling of his experiences with a little town named Flagstaff, in the months before it was to be flooded as part of a large lake for which a dam was being built. All improvements and repairs in the whole town were stopped. What was the use of painting a house if it were to be covered with water in six months? Why repair anything when the whole village was to be wiped out? So, week by week, the whole town became more and more bedraggled, more gone to seed, more woebegone. Then he added by way of explanation: "Where there is no faith in the future, there is no power in the present."[2]

8. You Are Invited To The Party

Have you ever felt left out of things? Maybe someone you knew gave a party and you weren't invited. But in Christ, you are invited to the party! Listen to that invitation as it comes from Paul in Ephesians 2:19-20: "Consequently, you are no longer foreigners and aliens, but fellow citizens with God's people and members of God's household, built on the foundation of the apostles and prophets, with Christ Jesus himself as the chief cornerstone." Did you catch that phrase, "no longer foreigners and aliens"? You are invited to be part of the family.

Each invitation comes with "RSVP" printed on the bottom. The Lord wants a response from you. What will you say?

9. Take Yourself Less Seriously

What a blow to learn that we are not the center of the universe! We strut around in our Hart, Schaffner, and Marx clothes thinking we are really something. The fact is we look more like Groucho, Harpo, and Chico Marx! It's a sobering day when we realize as we grow up that the world can get along without our control.

The biblical admonition is to take others more seriously and therefore ourselves less seriously. Paul wrote in Galatians 6:2-3, "Carry each other's burdens, and in this way you will fulfill the law of Christ. If anyone thinks he is something when he is nothing, he deceives himself."

10. Take God More Seriously

Spiritual life is a lot like a football game. Once in a great while we might make thirty yards on a long pass, but most of the time it is a grind to make inches. And those inches are won by sweat, pain, and great effort. But the point of spiritual growth is not how much progress you make. The point is that you are moving in the right direction.

An interesting man died in December of 1995. His name was Douglas Corrigan. In 1938 he took off in a single engine plane from New York heading for Long Beach, California. He landed 29 hours later in Dublin, Ireland! That flight earned him the nickname that stayed with him the rest of his life — "Wrong Way Corrigan." (I guess it's hard to stop and ask directions in a plane.)

When we take ourselves less seriously but God more seriously, we make some progress in the right direction. Read Paul's description of his struggles again from Romans 7:18-25. His hope is not in his own effort, but in the grace of God.

And so it is with all of us. As we face a new year, let us live with grace and faith. We have considered these ten theological affirmations for a new year:

1. Live your faith today because that is all we're promised.
2. Respect the past but don't live there.
3. If it's right, do it; if it's wrong, avoid it.
4. Everybody is carrying a heavy load. Be kind.
5. The only things that last are spiritual realities.
6. God really loves you.
7. Look forward in faith.
8. You are invited to the party.
9. Take yourself less seriously.
10. Take God more seriously.

May your new year be filled with the grace of God and the strength to overcome all obstacles.

---

1. *Parade*, Oct. 29, 1995, p.5.

2. Halford Luccock, *Unfinished Business* (New York: Harper and Brothers, 1956), p. 54.

Meaning Of The Magi

An Epiphany Sermon

Matthew 2:1-12

Some Christians in the world finished celebrating Christmas in January. For some of our brothers, January 6 is the high point of the Christmas season because that day is called Epiphany. Epiphany means "manifestation" and January 6 was the date the early church settled on as the time the wise men arrived in Bethlehem from the east. Jesus has come, and now the significance of his coming begins to be made clear. Jesus' life becomes "manifest." Twelfth Night, the evening before Epiphany, became in the early Church a time of merry-making which marked the end of the Christmas season. A cake was prepared and eaten each of the twelve days of Christmas — from December 25 until January 6. The Twelfth Cake was an ornamental cake, containing a bean or a coin. Whoever got the bean or the coin became the "King" of the festivities. You've heard of "King" cakes at Mardi Gras, and this is the same concept.

The Wise Men, or Magi as they are called, came to find the Christ child. In our church Christmas pageants we usually have them around the manger with the shepherds and angels and Mary and Joseph. But this clearly did not happen. Look at verse 11: "On coming to the house, they saw the child with his mother Mary ..." They were already in a house, and not in the cattle stall. We do not know exactly how long after the birth the Magi came. It could have been a couple of weeks, or even a year. We simply do not know, but it does not matter. What does matter is that they came.

Epiphany means "manifestation." If we listen closely to the story of the Magi, we will find out what was manifest, or made clear.

I. The Coming Of The Magi Pointed Out God's Open Hand

Have you ever felt like an outsider looking in? Have you ever felt left out, or ignored, or intentionally suppressed? Maybe it was

31

at school where you felt you just weren't one of the "in," group, or perhaps at work where you feel that everyone else is getting recognition and promotions while you get left behind. If you have ever felt this way, then you know how many people of the world felt before the coming of Christ. Think about it. Ancient Israel had been called by God to be a blessing to the whole world by telling everyone about the goodness of God. They were to be a "Light to the Nations." But what happened? The Jews had begun to see themselves as special in their own right, as chosen for blessing rather than as chosen for witness. If the Jews had a monopoly on God, what was everyone to do? There was a tension between the "haves" and the "have nots."

This tension is the background of Matthew 2. The Jews, the "haves," put in an appearance here. They were the ones with the Law, the prophets, the supposed blessing of God. But they were not watching for the coming of the Messiah. Look at verses 4 and 5. The chief priests and teachers of the law knew about the prophecy of Micah about Bethlehem. But the implication is that they were not watching, and that they did not care. That is not so hard to understand, is it? Every one of you owns the most significant book ever written — the Bible. Yet how many of you read it this week? I do not mean glanced at it enough to allow you to put a check on your Sunday school envelope. I mean really read this old book with the view toward getting something significant out of it? If you can plod along week after week with never a thought of the Scriptures, why can't we see how the people in Palestine twenty centuries ago did virtually the same thing? They grew dull in their diligence and apathetic in their apprehension of truth. The "haves," the ones who were God's chosen, were not on their spiritual guard.

On the other hand, the Magi from the east also make an appearance in this passage. The significance is found in their place of origin and their nationality. They were from non-Jewish lands and of a non-Hebrew nationality. Here were the "have nots," the Gentiles, who were searching for the Messiah. Verse 10 says, "When they saw the star, they were overjoyed." They had seen his star and they wanted to know who he was so they could worship him. People who might not have been expected to come or to care were the very ones who showed up on the doorstep of God's nursery and asked, "Can we rock the baby?"

Do you see what that means? In Christ, God had displayed his open hand to all men and women. Do you know why people shake hands as a sign of greeting? An open hand is a gesture that neither person has a weapon. The hand is open and the person can be trusted. The Magi came to find the Messiah and discovered that God was ready to shake hands with the whole world. God was ready to say, "I have no weapon, no hidden threat, no out-of-sight danger. All I have is my son, a baby in Bethlehem, who will call all men and women to me."

This is pure and simple gospel — essential good news! God declares his love for us. He promises a cure for our deepest malady, our sin. He states his open acceptance of us. Do you know this acceptance in your own life? It is not too late to find it, you know.

The Magi came to worship the Christ child. It was and is a manifestation of God's open hand. But there is more.

II. The Magi Also Show Humankind's Open Heart

When we sing, "We Three Kings," we might not be accurate. The Magi were learned men, perhaps primitive scientists and astrologers, but probably not kings. What they were is of less importance than what they did. What they did was have an open heart toward God.

You see, they made their pilgrimage for a purpose. They wanted to worship the one they felt was God-in-person, the Messiah. In so doing they displayed an open heart toward God. That was actually the first gift they had for the Christ child — a recognition of the insurmountable worth of God's son. This is where all genuine religious devotion begins — in the heart of one who looks up to God and says, "I need you and I choose you." This recognition was the result of waiting and watching, of longing and yearning, of hoping and praying. These Magi had long been on the lookout for the special occurrence which would forever change human life.

There is a key for our faith, too. A general law of the universe is that you usually get what you want, and you find what you are searching for. Thomas Edison wanted to make a new kind of light, so he began experimenting with different kinds of filaments. Thousands of failures later he finally hit upon that right combination of materials and environment to enable his light to work. Madam Curie wanted to learn the mysteries of a newly discovered substance called radium. She and her husband kept working and experimenting until they unlocked the secrets of that luminous mystery.

People who keep trying and working and thinking, regardless of the field, usually succeed. This is true in any field: science, sports, religion, or anything else. When you have a passion for life, a zest for living, an inner force that pushes you ahead, you can achieve your dreams. This is one thing the Magi teach us. They had an open heart toward God that gave them a determination to find the Messiah no matter what. Their journey was by way of express camel, not the most pleasant of treks. No one subsidized the trip. They paid for it themselves. No one gave them a map. They followed the star and their own inner compass. The major thing they had was a recognition that something had happened and whatever it was, they were determined to find out what it was.

That determination judges us. You and I often lack it. We want everything delivered to us on the proverbial silver platter. We have all sorts of things, but seem to lack one thing — a passionate, open heart toward God. Mark's Gospel tells of a rich young man who came to Jesus and asked what he must do to inherit eternal life. Jesus answered him, "One thing you lack. Go sell all you have and give the money to the poor and come follow me." What did that young fellow lack? It was this — a passionate, open heart toward God!

The Magi brought gifts to Christ. There were three gifts, and that gave rise to the speculation that there must have been three wise men. Later legends even assigned names to the men — Caspar, Melchior, Balthasar. They brought gold, frankincense, and myrrh.

Gold was a gift fit for a king. This king had no credentials, no throne, no large group, no army, no crown, nothing by way of worldly goods except a father and mother who wanted every good thing for their little son. But the Magi gave gold as their recognition that here was one worthy of the best. What do you suppose Jesus did with that gold? I'm sure he used it later to support his aging mother. Remember that Jesus said, "Do not store up for your-selves treasures on earth, where thieves break in and steal. But store up for yourselves treasures in heaven ..." (Matthew 6:19). What have you given to God lately which is befitting his kingship over your life?

Frankincense was a kind of perfume, an incense which was used in Jewish worship as an offering to God. It was a symbol that the Magi were wise indeed because they recognized that in the baby Jesus, God was somehow involved. What sweet offering have you lifted to God lately which speaks of his Lordship?

Myrrh was a resin substance which had several uses but was best known as an embalming spice. What a strange gift to give. Would someone go to a baby shower and give a coffin? But that, too, was a fitting offering for the Christ child. His life was not to be lived for himself alone, but was to be offered to God as a sacrifice for the many. From the beginning, then, his life was reckoned as belonging to God. What gift have you given to God lately which underscores the dedication of your life to him?

The Wise Men sought the Messiah to offer gifts because they found themselves rich toward God. They recognized that God had an open hand toward men. This also made them have an open heart toward God, as well as toward other people. When we consider the Magi, we find ourselves on a pilgrimage, too.

Have you seen any special stars lately?

The Word Is Near You

Romans 10: 5-13

Hear this ancient Japanese parable. Once there was a poor stone-cutter who owned nothing but his chisel, his hammer, a small bamboo hut, a ceramic rice bowl, and a pair of wooden chopsticks. He was too poor to marry, and he ate alone every day of the rice doled out to him by his employer's wife. His clothes were made of rags.

One day he saw a samurai warrior ride by the stone quarry on a fine horse, and he saw that the warrior was wearing beautiful red silk clothing like he had never seen. The stonecutter lamented out loud how he had not fine silk to clothe his body, and his cry carried to the heavens. So the heavens clothed him in red silk, and placed the new samurai in the court of the emperor.

One day, while in procession in the company of the emperor, the samurai noticed that only the emperor had a golden parasol held over his head. He lamented that the emperor was more powerful than he, and the heavens heard his cry. The samurai was made the emperor.

In the heat of the summer the emperor noticed how the sun scorched everything with its hot rays. He realized he was not the most powerful being, so he wished to be the sun. The heavens heard his cry and made him the sun. He directed his power, heat, and light everywhere, and scorched the earth.

But one day he noticed that a cloud placed itself between the earth and himself, and he could not send his rays wherever he wished. He realized that something was more powerful than he, so he wished to be the cloud. The heavens heard his cry and he became the cloud. He blocked the sun's rays and sent floods upon the earth. Everything yielded to his power.

Everything, that is, except one. A rock would not yield to his force. No matter how much water fell, the rock would not budge. So he cried out once again that he wished to be the rock, and the heavens heard his cry. He became the rock and did not budge when the sun shone upon him and the clouds rained upon him.

But one day a man who had a hammer and a chisel came. The man hewed stone out of the great rock, and the rock cried that there was one more powerful than he, so he wished to become that man. The heavens heard his cry and he was made a stonecutter. Day after day he cut small stones from great rocks, and it was very hard labor. All he owned was a hammer and a chisel, a small bamboo hut, some ragged clothing, a ceramic rice bowl, and a pair of wooden chopsticks. But he was now happy.[1]

Or was he? The ancient parable ends here, but I think the cycle kept going, don't you? The human heart is a reckless and restless prodigal. It is a wild mustang straining against every rope which tries to subdue it. It is a garden which brings forth every manner of weed and thistle which chokes the delicate flowers and tender shoots.

It is this wild, reckless heart that God is after. The testimony of the entire Bible is that God searches for hearts, but even God has trouble with us because we are so fickle.

The other side of this is that man has tried to find God, too. "Man is incurably religious," we are told. And so he is, so we are. In times past people have ransacked the universe searching for God. They recited incantations or burned incense or spilled blood, all in an effort to find God. And all the while, God was close by to be found. This is what Paul is saying in Romans 10. "The word is near you," he says. "It is in your mouth and in your heart."

I. The Word Is Near You: You Don't Have To Bring Him Down
Paul had been around. He knew the efforts of people to squeeze Christ into molds of their own making. It had gone on from the beginning. The Twelve wanted Jesus to act "normal." Herod and Pilate wanted him to be an "ordinary" criminal. The Christians in Corinth were confused about gifts and sex, and wanted to shape Christ to fit their distorted sense of right. The Christians in Colossae were troubled about the power of the stars and tried to fit Christ into the confused theology.

And today? Jesus has been made into everything from a radical revolutionary to Superstar to ascetic hermit. But Paul's insight for his day is as contemporary as a computer. "The word is near you." We need not try to pull Christ from heaven. He has already come! This is great news. Our task or responsibility is therefore not to try to earn his love or attract his notice.

We need not bribe God! The Word is near you, and you do not need to bring Christ down. He is already here. This is not a command to find the Savior or get to work, or even to show up at church every time the doors open. It is a promise of Christ's presence in your life, no matter what.

Generations of our ancient ancestors did all sorts of things to catch God's attention and earn his love. They burned incense and slaughtered animals. They bruised and beat their own bodies. They treated others harshly, thinking it was God's will. All of this was done to earn his care. But Paul says that we need not do anything to earn God's care. We already have it! The word is near you. You do not have to bring Christ down.

II. The Word Is Near You: You Don't Have To Raise Christ Up

Christ is not the representation of a distant, unreachable God. But neither is he a dead prophet. Jesus lived with all the verve, strength, and integrity which any man has ever known. His life was neither decoy nor sham. It was as real as yours and mine. In the same manner, his death was not a fake. When Jesus was spiked to a cross, the blood that dripped onto the soil was real. His life was snuffed out like a candle in a storm. But on the third day that flame was rekindled, and it shines today in the heart of every person who will flee the darkness.

God is with his people in all circumstances. He is alive, and we need not spend our time trying to resurrect him as if he were dead. He is in this world working with people in events both ordinary and unusual. Consider this event. A Christian missionary was taking a flight from Nairobi, Kenya, to Mombassa. About fifteen minutes into the flight one engine died and the other was having trouble. Just prior to this, the missionary had struck up a conversation with a man seated across the aisle him. This man was an German tourist who was not interested in religion. "I don't have time for that," he told the missionary. But as the plane began to loose altitude he changed his mind! When the plane leveled out this man jumped across the aisle, grabbed the missionary by the arm and said, "Now, you tell me how to be saved." The Christian explained simply how to receive Christ, and the tourist knelt in the aisle and asked Christ to come into his life. When the plane safely landed a few minutes later, this man began to speak in German to the other tourists with him. Before long eighteen others prayed to receive salvation through Christ.

The word is near you. You do not have to bring him up.

III. The Word Is Near You: You Can Confess His Presence In Your Life

Hear again Paul's promise in Romans 10: "If you confess with your mouth, 'Jesus is Lord,' and believe in your heart that God raised him from the dead, you will be saved." A meaningful confession is an expression of what is in the heart. To confess Christ is to express belief in both words and especially in significant action.

The Christian Church has spent twenty centuries fighting over words. Some of this is right, because the Church needs correct theology, and proper language in which to express that theology. But much of the squabbles have been of little consequence, other than diverting effort from the genuine work of doing what Christ called the Church to do.

Confession of Christ is the life of the Church. It is life lived in harmony with God. Paul's call for confession is based on the fact that God has given himself to humankind in love through Christ. When one lives in harmony with that love, he is confessing Christ. When she does not live in such harmony, she is denying Christ.

An acquaintance recently called me from Seattle, Washington. I was surprised to hear from him because I had not spoken to him in over fifteen years. This is the story he told me. He had started a Christian coffeehouse to witness to students at a large university in Louisiana. This is where I had gotten to know him. Things went well for a year or so, but people began to lose interest, donations dropped off, and he finally gave up in disgust. This man was angry — angry at people, angry at the university, and especially angry at God. He packed up his family and moved as far from Louisiana as he could get — thus, Seattle. In his conversation to me, he said, "I have been running from God for fifteen years. And I just got tired of running. I recently began praying and attending church again, and for the first time in fifteen years I feel as if my life is on target again."

The word is near you. Are you running, or angry, or hurt?

The word is near you. Are you trying to resurrect Christ from the dead in order to have him do something in your life?

The word is near you. Are you scurrying around trying to earn his love?

How near is the word? A baby bird was heard to ask its mother, "Mother, what is air?" To this she made no reply but spread her wings and flew. A baby fish asked its mother, "Mother, what is water?" She made no reply but swished her tail and swam. A baby ant asked its mother, "Mother, what is dirt?" She made no reply but stretched her legs and dug the burrow a little deeper. A child in a nursery asked her mother, "Mother, what is love?" She made no reply but picked up the child and hugged her.[2]

Like water to a fish; like air to a bird; like dirt to an ant; like love to a child. So is the presence of the word — God himself — to those who love him. The word is near you.

---

1. Adaptation of an ancient Japanese tale told in *Storyfest Ministry Magazine*, Vol. 1, pp. 3-4.

2. From a suggestion by Edward E. Thornton, "Awaking Consciousness: The Psychological Reality in Christ-Consciousness," in *Review and Expositor*, Vol. 76, No. 2 (Spring 1979), p. 185.

The Light Of Your Life

John 12:34-36; 42-50

This was the beginning of the end. With these words Jesus had no more to say to the public crowds. From then on he spoke only to small groups of his followers, but not to the people in general. The crowds had heard the message and had seen the miracles. Most were interested, some believed, and a few even followed Jesus. But for the most part they did not care enough to make a difference.

The religious leaders, the Pharisees and Sadducees, had heard the logic of his teachings, and had felt the force of his God-centered personality. They had tried to trap him and had plotted against him. They, too, had witnessed the signs of his authority, but instead of believing, they became more set in their opposition to Jesus. When all was said and done they did not want a prophetic word from God. They cared nothing for the message of God which came as a light to a darkened world. What the religious leaders really wanted was for God to bless their stranglehold on the synagogue, to okay their interpretation of their Scriptures, and to give the nod of approval for their ethics. The last thing many of them wanted was for some prophet to come along preaching love and justice. The very idea!

So the days of the crowds and the accolades were drawing to a close, and everyone seemed somehow to know it. The crowds dwindled and the accolades turned into a collective "ho hum." Had you or I been in Jesus' sandals we probably would have thrown up our hands in despair and said, "Well, if this is the way you're going to act, you can just forget the whole thing."

Thank God neither we nor anyone like us were in Jesus' place. Instead of shaking the dust off his feet and telling the human race to go to hell, Jesus never quit. Verse 44 puts this in unusual words: "Then Jesus cried out...." The miracles had made only a temporary impact on the people. The authoritative word from the Lord himself left some people cold. But Jesus never gave up.

43

When all seems to have been said and done, when everything seems to have had "The End" stamped on it, Jesus cried out, "I have come into the world as a light, so that no one who believes in me should stay in darkness." Here were his last words for the public. "I have come as a light and no one needs to live in the darkness anymore."

People do not need to be religious or even have a church background to understand Jesus here. The world for so many people is a dark and dangerous place. Many seem to live in the dark, to have their minds blackened by their refusal to live in the light. A woman came to my office in another state one day and briefly told me her story. Her husband had been an alcoholic and regularly beat her up. She finally divorced him for her own sanity, but then the children refused to have anything to do with her. She lived alone in a bleak house staring through blank windows into a bleak future. She asked as tears welled up in her eyes, "Why does it have to be this way?" She did not want an answer, of course. She just wanted someone to hear her out and say, "I care about you." But the question is still relentless. "Why is it this way?" Let's explore it for a moment.

I. Life Is Black When We Choose To Live In Darkness

Verses 47-48 hold before our eyes the frightening reality of moral judgment. "As for the person who hears my words but does not keep them, I do not judge him. For I did not come to judge the world but to save it." So what is the judgment? Look at verse 48: "There is a judge for the one who rejects me and does not accept my words; that very word which I spoke will condemn him at the last day." I think Jesus' words here refer to the end of time, but I know they pertain to the here and the now, too. It is simply an inviolable law of the universe that if we try to slap God in the face it is we who suffer the pain. If a person acts as if he is his own master he finds sooner or later that he is a slave to something. To choose the darkness over the light is to go stumbling through life with bruised toes and a bruised heart.

Look at the Pharisees in this passage. John tells us that some of them actually believed in Jesus but were afraid to acknowledge

44

it. Why? They feared being put out of the synagogue, "for they loved the praise from men more than praise from God." They chose institutional security over sacred truth. They chose personal prestige over faithful following.

This is always a mistake. The word *prestige* comes from a Latin word which means an illusion or a juggler's tricks. That's what prestige is — an illusion, a trick. And they chose that over God!

Routine and habit are powerful task masters. When we do something over and over again we learn it deeply. A child plays scales up and down the piano keyboard even when she would rather tackle something with rhythm. A college student writes out foreign words again and again in order to let them become part of him. An athlete practices his moves on the gridiron many times so he will not have to think about them consciously on game day. Habits in this sense can be helpful and positive.

But we all know that the threads of a habit can become a steel cable. We can reject the light so long it becomes a habit, a terrible habit. Lon Chaney, Sr. starred as the villain in the classic movie, *The Hunchback of Notre Dame.* He said that he had to strap himself in a harness and tie himself hunched over in order to look like a genuine hunchback. But as the days of the filming stretched into weeks, Chaney found that the longer he stayed in the stooped over position, the longer he took to stand up straight after the day's filming. His body was getting used to being bent over.

This happens morally, too. A person can choose to stay bent over morally instead of standing up straight in Christ. One can choose the darkness and live more like an animal than a human being made in God's image. I have a cousin who died at age 39 of DT's brought on by alcohol abuse. His last days were spent strapped down in a hospital bed hallucinating about snakes and people who wanted to hurt him. When you continually choose darkness, sooner or later you lose the ability to see the light.

Some of you might have visited some of the caves in central Tennessee. On one of the tours visitors are shown some small fish which have lived in the dark caves for generations. As the eons have passed the fish have simply lost their eyes. They lived in the dark so long they finally lost their ability to see.

Many of the people in Jesus' day had been in the darkness so long they just could not, or would not, see the light. Some followed, certainly, but so many turned their backs and hardened their hearts. "They loved the praise of man more than the praise of God." Isn't that sad? It was in Jesus' day, and still is! The refusal to believe, or the shallowness of belief, brings moral darkness. It discolors and shrouds life. The apostle Paul spoke of such a person as a "natural" or "carnal" man. This is the person who closes his eyes to the truth and says, "I don't care what anybody says, I'm going to do it my way!"

Life seems black and bleak when people choose to live in the darkness. But the other side is just as true:

II. Life Is Illuminated When We Choose To Live In The Light

Jesus said, "I have come into the world as a light, so that no one who believes in me should stay in darkness." Did you catch that? We do not have to live in the darkness. The darkness of a cave is all right for a bat, but human beings are not bats. We are made for the light. Some psychologists are discovering that some people who suffer from chronic depression simply fail to get enough light. A part of the treatment includes installing brighter lights in the depressed person's home, and having this person go outside more often.

God gave us eyes to perceive. But more importantly, he gave us a mind and a heart to respond to the light which comes our way in Christ. His light is truth. My wife and I have visited Mammoth Cave in Kentucky on several occasions. Twice we have gone into the largest cavern several hundred feet underground. The guard points out the extensive system of electric lights in the cave, and then, after a warning, shuts them off. The blackness is so thick and total it is disorienting. I have heard of darkness so complete you could not see your hand in front of your face, but that was the only time I have ever experienced it. After a few seconds of this complete blackout the guard lights one match. One tiny match can light up that entire cavern of thousands of square feet. On those occasions I have always remembered what John says about Jesus at the beginning of his Gospel: "The light shines in the darkness, and the darkness has not overcome it."

This is true with Jesus' followers as we live in his light. An elderly woman showed this to be true in her life. Her eyesight was getting worse, and her glasses were not doing her much good, so she went to her ophthalmologist. The doctor could not find much to encourage her about her eyes. To his surprise, she did not seem upset. She told him about all the wonderful things God had done in her life: how she had a great husband, loving children, and a meaningful church. Her sight was getting worse but she was not going to fret over that. The doctor listened to all of this for a while and then said, "Your eyesight is poor, but your vision is better than perfect." Here was a woman who had lived in the light all of her life, and even in old age she found that her life was still bright because of God.

Jesus had said that no one who believes in him should stay in the darkness. That message had gotten through to a few people in his day. We read verses 42 and 43 earlier. They said that most of the leaders of the people who did believe were afraid to say so. But jump ahead toward the close of John's Gospel. In chapter 19, verses 38 and 39, we see something remarkable. Joseph and Nicodemus had been "closet" disciples, but the death of Jesus brought them out into the open. They had seen the immortal light shine in their own lives, and were determined not to remain in the dark. To live in the light means to put belief into practice.

My wife and I spent a few weeks at Mansfield College in Oxford, England, several years ago. One afternoon we noticed a small black cross on the sidewalk beside one of the major streets. We stopped to see what it was and this is what we found out. Two men had been burned at the stake on that spot in 1555. These men were Hugh Latimer and Nicholas Ridley. They were influenced by the thinking of the Protestant reformers. They broke from the Church of England and tried to establish what we today would call a Protestant church. For their trouble they were sentenced to be burned at the stake. Onlookers took down their last words. This is what Bishop Latimer said: "Be of good comfort, Master Ridley, and play the man. We shall this day light such a candle by God's grace in

England as I trust shall never be put out." He was right. The light that shone through their lives is still shining today in this church. There were two men who put belief into practice. They had seen the light of God in the face of Jesus Christ, and they would not back down for anything!

You and I have only two choices in life. We can hide in the caves of our own making and exist in the darkness. But be sure you understand what this means. It means ultimate defeat, because, as Jesus said, "There is a judge for the one who rejects me and does not accept my words; that very word which I spoke will condemn him at the last day." If a person really, really wants to stay in the darkness, he can. God lets him.

The second choice is that we can follow the light as it comes in Christ. This means believing, but more than that it means acting on our beliefs — in other words, living like one who has been changed in Christ.

Robert Louis Stevenson looked out of his window one evening many years ago. Those were the days before electric lights. Stevenson saw the town lamplighter coming along. As this lamplighter lit the street lamps in succession, Stevenson was impressed at the sight. He wrote about the lamplighter who went along "punching holes in the darkness."

Jesus Christ came into this world as a light, and he punched holes in the darkness. Has he done that in your life? He can, you know. You need only ask his presence in your life, and live in his light. Why live in darkness when the light is available?

A Collision Of Kingdoms
John 18:33-37

The New Testament is full of stories about events which seem turned around, backward, upside down, even ironic. Such is the narrative of Jesus standing before Pilate. The Pharisees had trumped up charges against Jesus and had accused him of blasphemy and treason. These were two separate charges. The accusation of blasphemy was a religious charge sure to turn the common people against him. After all, how many people would follow a leader who blasphemed against God? The second charge of treason was supposed to turn the political leaders against Jesus. How could they allow him to continue if he was plotting the overthrow of Rome?

So Pilate found himself in quite a dilemma. He had on his hands a prisoner who was accused of disloyalty to the Jews' religious traditions and disloyalty to Pilate's political power. What do you do with such a man as this?

The answer to this question brings us to today's text. Jesus was taken before Pilate after his arrest. His accusers, the Jews, would not even enter the palace to bring their charges against him. They wanted to be able to eat the Passover and would have become ceremonially unclean had they gone into Pilate's palace. They did not mind condemning an innocent man to death, but they did not want to become soiled for the ceremony! Verse 31 shows us that they had already made up their minds to execute Jesus. They just did not want to get dirty doing it.

So Pilate, the so-called ruler, found himself being a glorified lackey. He shuttled back and forth between the Jews outside and Jesus inside. This is the great irony — almost comedy — of this narrative. Pilate was supposed to represent everything of the kingdom of imperial Rome — authority, power, wealth, and if necessary, the ability to shed blood. And look at the one he was questioning that day — Jesus. Jesus was representative of a kingdom, too. But his kingdom was not advanced by ruthless men. His kingdom had no authority to twist arms and spill blood. It had no wealth but the hearts and minds of men and women.

So Jesus and Pilate stood there facing each other in the imperial palace so long ago. Pilate shuttled back and forth between the inner chamber where he questioned Jesus and the outer courtyard where the accusers were. The poor man could not even see that he was being manipulated by them. He was supposed to be the leader, the one in charge. Yet he failed miserably.

When he could not figure out what else to do, Pilate questioned Jesus. Look at the session. Jesus — the so-called prisoner — is firmly in control in John's account of this meeting. Pilate asks, "Are you the king of the Jews?" He gets no direct answer but only a counter question: "Is that your own idea or did others talk to you about me?" What sort of answer is that? It flusters Pilate and he shoots back with all the bravado he can muster, "Am I a Jew?" He is so afraid of losing his kingdom. Poor man. He cannot even see that he is looking at the embodiment of another kind of kingdom, a kingdom built on the Lordship of God and the principle of love of neighbor.

"My kingdom is not of this world," Jesus says. Yes, there it is — both an admission of guilt and a protest of innocence. Jesus admitted that he was the king of his kingdom. For the Jews this was blasphemy and for Pilate a serious threat to his power. But neither had heard what Jesus really said: "My kingdom is not of this world." Two kingdoms collided in their presence, and nobody even heard the crunch!

Pilate had the armies and the cash and the power, yet he was helpless as an infant when face to face with Jesus. The swords and the treasury meant nothing when stacked up against a solitary figure who was looking beyond the confines of this sad world. "My kingdom is not of this world." It is a word that still needs to be sounded today.

When the church today wants to be "powerful" or "victorious" it had better take heed as to just what it means. Power and victory are always idols which drain the church and misdirect its path. The church that wants to be "victorious" in this world will lose its soul. For this reason, Christians today must keep the vigil against the lust for power and victory at the expense of service, love, and forgiveness.

Long ago Pilate questioned Jesus. That meeting marked the collision of two kingdoms. Pilate is dead and dust. Ancient Rome is but a mention in the history books. But Jesus Christ is alive and his kingdom is still spreading in the lives of women and men who give him their allegiance. There is no real question as to which kingdom outlived the other. The question for us is, "Which shall we serve?"

Life's Central Issue

Deuteronomy 6:1-9

These words come as the "commands," "decrees," and "laws" which are given by God for his people. The hearers are told to listen, obey, and then teach them to others. The first hearers of these words were the ancient Hebrews of Israel. They had this word delivered to them as the supreme word by which to live.

Jesus quoted this passage many centuries later. He, too, made this the supreme word of religious life. A man, identified as a teacher of the law, asked Jesus what the greatest commandment was. Jesus quoted from Deuteronomy 6. The teacher then responded positively to Jesus' answer. To this Jesus said, "You are not far from the kingdom of God."

What was so important about this teaching from Deuteronomy 6? This section of Scripture tells us about the nature of God, the necessity of love, and the priority of faith. They all help move us toward life's central issue which is this: "To whom do we belong?"

Let us consider these concepts that move us closer to the truth.

I. The Nature Of God

"Hear, O Israel: The Lord our God, the Lord is one." This was a startling word to the ancient Hebrews. They lived in a world of many gods. Ra, Tiamat, and Apsu were just some of the names of the gods of the ancient near east. Some of the neighbors of Israel believed there were gods of the earth, of the sky, and of the sea. There were gods aplenty! Even centuries later the apostle Paul encountered such thinking. Look at 1 Corinthians 8:5-6. To Paul's ancestors there was one name which stood out above all the other false gods — Baal. Baal was seen by some people as the god of nature. As such, they thought he was responsible for fertility, for the weather, for the growth of the crops, among other things. But listen again to Deuteronomy 6: "The Lord is one." Did you catch that? One God, the Lord. God's nature is oneness, unity.

This calls for undivided loyalty and allegiance to this Lord. You see, there is not one God for Sunday, and another for Monday through Saturday. If God is sovereign on Sunday morning, then he is during the rest of the week, too.

God is one, and therefore you and I are called on to love and serve him with undivided allegiance. Aesop told the story of a lamb which was chased by a wolf. It ran into a temple. The wolf said, "The priest will slay you on the altar if he catches you." The lamb replied, "Perhaps, but it is better to be sacrificed to God than to be devoured by a wolf."

Deuteronomy 6 helps us face up to life's central question about our allegiance. The question is, "To whom do we belong?" The answer is, "We belong to the Lord in undivided devotion."

II. The Necessity Of Love

This word comes, too: "Love the Lord your God with all your heart and with all your soul and with all your strength." We belong to one Lord in undivided loyalty. This means that we serve God through loving him and by loving other people. This is what the church is all about. It is the lighthouse which proclaims the love of God for people, and calls for people to love God in return.

We are called on to love with all our heart, soul, and strength. This was the way the ancient Hebrew had of speaking of a total person. This is a call to love and serve God with the whole of our beings — mind, body, spirit — everything we have and everything that we are.

To whom do we belong? We belong to God with an undivided loyalty and love him with everything we have.

III. The Priority Of Faith

We are also called to share this faith in God. This faith is spelled out in verses 6-9. It is to be heartfelt. The Scripture says to write the commands upon our hearts. It is to be personal. Verse 7 says that this faith is to be at the heart of a person's life. It is to be among the topics of conversation at home and with the children. Faith in God, in other words, is not reserved just for Sunday at church. And this faith in God is to be shared. "Impress them upon your children," we are told. This points out the responsibility of parents or guardians.

Everyone needs to know the answer to life's central question — to whom do I belong? Our text for today helps us answer that question. We belong to the single Lord whom we serve with undivided loyalty and know through personal faith.

If you do not know these answers yet, don't you think it's time you did?

The Serious Business
Of Following Jesus
Luke 9:57-62

A story is told about a small town on the border of Canada and the United States. For years both countries had fought over the ownership of the town. Finally, the matter was brought to court and the judge decided in favor of the USA. The town was definitely in America. At the end of the trial an old fellow was heard to say as he left the courtroom, "Oh, thank goodness. I just don't think I could have stood another one of those cold Canadian winters."

Isn't it strange how a shift in perspectives can change so many things? An American winter sounds milder than a Canadian one. Think of how life looks different when you are 35 as compared to 21, or 65 compared to 35. The angle from which we look at things determines much of what we see.

The encounter of three men during the travels of Jesus is a story of shifting perspectives. Each of the men was invited to look at life from a different angle, to see it afresh, to see the dangerous side as well as the inviting side. As such, it is an invitation for us to reconsider this serious business of following Jesus.

Consider these dangers:

I. The Danger Of Impulsive Decisions

Jesus and his group were trekking down the road toward Jerusalem. Jesus had "set his face" toward the Holy City, determined to go there come what may. Along the way a volunteer presented himself and said, "I'll follow you anywhere." That was easy enough to understand. A sense of excitement over Jesus and the disciples hung like a canopy, but the volunteer did not realize that it was more like a shroud than a circus tent. Everybody wants to join the circus, but who wants to join a funeral procession?

"I'll follow you anywhere." Here are four small words which seem to sum up the dedication of a man's whole life. But Jesus was too wise to take such a commitment at face value. Matthew calls this volunteer a "scribe." As such he was one of the leading men, a stable person, a pillar of the community. Jesus' statement was a way of asking this stable, secure, established person if he could really handle homelessness, instability, insecurity, and disestablishment. How would a man who belonged to a leading law firm handle being an itinerant follower? How could one who was so much at home with the Torah, the law, deal with the radically new way which Jesus was reinterpreting it?

"Foxes have holes, and birds of the air have nests; but the Son of man has nowhere to lay his head." "Sir, if you join this group you must realize that you will have less stability than the creatures of the air and land. Your bed will be the ground; your pillow, the garments you carry with you; your roof, the sky. Are you sure you can follow like this?"

Hopping on "bandwagons" is no new pastime. It is as ancient as the scribe who encountered Jesus on the road to Jerusalem. It is based on spur-of-the-moment decisions, a desire to get into the act. But jumping to hasty conclusions can result in spiritual stone bruises. The scribe simply had not thought it through! To follow Jesus meant sharing his homelessness and rejection. Could he do that? Indeed, can we?

I often feel that we sing our hymns mechanically without realizing the import of what they express. Take the old favorite, "Footsteps of Jesus." Hear with fresh ears what it says:

> *Tho they lead o'er the cold, dark mountains,*
> *Seeking his sheep,*
> *Or along by Siloam's fountains,*
> *Helping the weak.*
> *If they lead thro' the temple holy,*
> *Preaching the Word,*
> *Or in homes of the poor and lowly,*
> *Serving the Lord.*

"Foxes have holes.... Are you sure you want to get involved in this?"

I once had a job selling vacuum cleaners door to door. My boss gave me training on how to sell these contraptions. I was to demonstrate it, get the buyer excited about it, and get her to sign a contract for it immediately. "Take advantage of her impulsive wants," the boss would say. This is exactly why some states now have laws giving buyers a "cooling off" period where they can think about what they've done and cancel a contract if they want to.

Impulsive decisions in religion cause problems, too. Revival meetings are necessary and good, but we have to be careful about pressuring people to do something they really don't want to do. Jesus did not say anything like, "We'll sing just one more verse. Won't you come now?" Instead, he asked the volunteer if he could pay the cost of following. Earnestness and enthusiasm are necessary ingredients in our religious faith. But enthusiasm and earnestness all by themselves are not enough. They must be coupled with will and linked to action. Mark Twain once recorded in his journal: "Campbellite revival. All converted except me. All sinners again in a week."

Jeremy Taylor used to speak of the biblical meaning of prudence which is, as he put it, "reason's girdle and passion's bridle." Jesus' call for disciples is, among other things, a call for such a girdle and a bridle. "I'll follow you anywhere." It's so easy to say, and so incredibly difficult to do! To accomplish it requires sacrificial living, giving up the less important to gain the most important. Christ has called you and me to that. How else could you explain the words, "Take up your cross and follow me"?

Even if we jump the hurdle of impulsive decisions, another problem presents itself immediately. It is borne out in the words of the man who said, "Lord, let me first go bury my father."

II. The Danger Of Reluctance

The first man volunteered. Now we see another, but a draftee. Jesus said to him, "Follow me." This was a straight-forward invitation to join the ranks of those ready to think through the invitation and join in, come what may. To such a draft the man makes a logical-sounding reply: "Let me first go and bury my father." Surely even Jesus could pause long enough for a funeral. He had done it before.

But there was a hitch here. Family customs of the ancient Near East stipulated that a son had a responsibility to a father as long as the elder man lived. When he died the younger man was responsible for arranging the burial. But in this case, no funeral procession was ready because no corpse was available. It seems likely that the father of this man to whom Jesus spoke was still very much alive. The fellow was putting Jesus off saying something like, "I need to stay here and attend to family responsibilities. When my father has died and I have taken care of my duties, then I will come with you."

We do not have to be geniuses to understand the meaning behind that reply. This young man was reluctant to follow, to get involved, to commit himself. "Better to play it safe," he thought, so a little excuse will do. As a pastor, I hear these all the time as I invite people to church. "Well, I'd come but I'm so crippled with arthritis that I just can't climb those steps." Then I see this person everywhere in town. Or, "I'd come but I'd miss Dr. Schuller on television" Or, "I just don't like all those hypocrites down there." Or, well, you name it, and I suppose I've heard it. Behind these thin veils stands the one and only reason. These people are reluctant to get involved with a cause above and beyond their own tiny worlds.

Jesus listened to the odd-sounding excuse: "Let me first bury my father." His reply seems on the surface to be just as odd: "Let the dead bury the dead. You go proclaim the kingdom." He shifted the perspective and pointed this out to the young man. "You are allowing your waiting for death to crowd out your living here and now. Go out and live."

For everything there is a crucial moment — a time when a person's whole being says, "Yes, the time is now!" To put some things off too long is to risk never doing them at all. For example, a man and woman come to love each other and plan to get married. They experience some difficulties in the relationship and postpone the wedding. After a while they reschedule it, but again have problems and postpone it. For some people this could go on and on. But with each postponement comes the danger that the wedding will never come off at all.

"Strike while the iron is hot" is an old proverb fit for blacksmiths and also for religious faith. There is a time for taking our time and thinking out actions and results. Remember that Jesus told the first volunteer to consider what he was getting into. But there is also a time for moving ahead once the consequences are considered. To fail to do so is to court potential disaster.

Many years ago a young man went to work at a hardware store. He found all sorts of junk that took up space but did not sell well. This clerk asked the owner to allow him to put it all on one table and sell each item for ten cents. He did so and had a successful sale. Later he did the same thing, and had another successful sale. The clerk approached the owner and suggested that they open up a store specializing in items that cost only a nickel or dime. The owner thought it was a bad idea and refused. The clerk went into business for himself and became very successful with his idea. His name was F. W. Woolworth. His old employer later said, "I have calculated that every word I used to turn young Woolworth down cost me about a million dollars."

This is true with religious commitments. Jesus wants his followers to consider what they are in for, but he does not want them to waste their lives over the matter without ever making up their minds. The all-consuming claim of Jesus is too important! Matters of the Kingdom of God just will not wait. Obedience is necessary when Jesus calls.

We expend great creativity in coming up with ways to get around the truth, or of obscuring it. I ran across a list of real estate terms used in selling houses, along with a "translation" for us lay people. Consider some of these:

Unobstructed view:	No trees
Waiting your imaginative touch:	Complete wreck
Handyman's dream:	Owner's nightmare
Pond site:	Swamp
Central to everything:	A very noisy area
Easy commuting:	Remote from everything
Charm all its own:	Don't lean on old porch rail
Needs finishing touches:	Needs roof
Rustic appeal:	Outdoor plumbing

We can do that kind of thing with our religious faith. There are creative ways of saying, "Let me bury my family." The only thing that moves us beyond this is obedience. Without this simple discipline a child burns his fingers on the stove after his mother tells him it is hot.

A child in school fails a test because she did not follow instructions. A marriage falls apart because the partners are not obedient to the rules of relationships which govern a marriage. A friendship crumbles because the two friends do not honor their mutual pact of honesty.

To this reluctant man, and to our reluctance, Jesus commands, "Let the dead bury the dead." Let those who have no spiritual insight or interest attend to these other matters, but you get out of your spiritually dead surroundings and follow me! Let those who have no sense of duty to the Kingdom meet the requirement of the Law. You join me now to overcome the power of death.

A volunteer is impulsive. A draftee is reluctant. A third man enters the picture. We don't know whether he volunteered or was called to join Jesus. All we know is his answer: "I will follow you, Lord; but let me first say farewell to those at my home." Here is a man who brings to our attention:

III. The Danger Of Indecisiveness

Once again the request seems logical. All he wanted was to say good-bye to the family. That should not take too long, should it? The time element was not the issue. Jesus knew that the issue was this man's double-mindedness, his inability to decide one way or the other. Indecisive people have a tough time following Christ. In fact, they have a tough time doing anything much. When I was growing up my best friend's mother was such a person. We would ask if my friend could come to my house to play. I can still see her as she would divert her eyes and whisper apologetically, "Well, I don't know. We better wait until his daddy gets home and ask him." That was her stock answer to every request. I realize now there was more to it than simple indecisiveness, but her inability to decide used to drive me crazy!

We hear from the lips of this third man in the narrative those two telling words: "But first ..." They indicate his indecision about what to do. I hear those words fairly often as I speak with people. I talk to a teenager about faith and am told, "Well, okay, but let me have some fun first." I talk to a young couple about becoming involved in the church. The answer comes something like this: "Yes, we will, but first let us get our children grown." I speak to a middle-aged couple and hear, "Sure, we're interested, but we have so many responsibilities now. We'll come when we get the house paid off and the kids out of college." I talk to an older adult and hear, "Absolutely! I'm going to start coming, but first let me get used to retirement and my new routine." You know what happens. By the time all the conditions of the "but first" reply are met, friends and family are walking behind that little box out to that unhappy place in the cemetery.

To all of this Jesus says, "No one who puts his hand to the plow and looks back is fit for the kingdom." Plows in his day had only one handle and they required the farmer's whole attention. Jesus was saying that the plowpoint was set and the team had been signaled to go. To wonder then would be to defeat the whole purpose. As with an ancient plow, your religious commitment needs single-minded, full attention. This is not the time for looking back to see what might have been. This is the time for looking squarely ahead to what is to come. Forget the excuses. Follow Christ!

When Cortez led his conquistadors into Mexico in search of gold and conquest, he burned his ships in the harbor. He did not want his soldiers mentally looking back over their shoulders at the way home. He left only one course — straight ahead. So it is with our faith.

Three men came along. One was impulsive and did not think through his actions. Another was reluctant and held back. A third was indecisive and could not seem to make up his mind. To all of these — to all of us — Jesus stands before us and waves us onward. He changes our perspective and straightens out our thinking. Our refusal to see life from his angle makes us similar to a woman in an ancient legend from India. This woman lived with her family in a rural area. Her husband was killed by a tiger one year. A son

63

was bitten by a cobra the next. A daughter was trampled by an elephant the next year. Finally someone asked her why she did not move to the city. She replied, "What? Don't you know that cities are dangerous?"

To go to Christ is dangerous. It will change us. But is that really worse than staying where we are now?

A Stubborn
Misunderstanding Of Prayer
Matthew 6:5-8

What does the word "prayer" bring to your mind? A regular meeting at church? A last-ditch effort to stave off some disaster? An intimate communication between you and God? All of these images, or others, might come to mind when we think of prayer. We will be considering many ideas about prayer in this small book. But sometimes we can tell what a thing is by discovering what it is not. This is true with prayer. If, at the very beginning of our study, we raise several popular ideas that are probably wrong, then we will be on our way toward discovering what prayer really is. Let me point out something here, though. These ideas about prayer are stubborn and keep cropping up in every generation. One major reason for this fact is that they are immature notions. New Christians especially are prone to believe these ideas. Often, when a person has a chance to grow and mature in relationship to Christ, prayer life will take on a deeper meaning.

I. Prayer Is Not A Lottery

A lottery is a game of chance. A person gambles that what he bets will reward his efforts by paying off more than the original bet. I do not mean to sound crass when I suggest that some people seem to think of prayer in this lottery fashion. They think, "Hey, I'll say a prayer in this situation. It couldn't hurt anything and it might pay off big."

This way of thinking is purely selfish. The sole motive behind the act is to gamble that a few words mumbled to the deity might "do some good." As you read the Bible you will find many prayers addressed to God. Many of those are said by people who were in trouble. They asked for help. The difference in that and the contemporary prayer-as-lottery view is this: the people in the Bible who prayed for help already had a relationship with God established. They are asking the help of the One whom they knew as the Lord. They were not just casting out verbiage in the hopes that it might possibly be heard by "the man upstairs" and answered affirmatively.

II. Prayer Is Not A Twist Of God's Arm

Another popular notion about prayer is that it is a way to make God do something he does not want to do. It is a way to twist God's arm to force him to do your will. Most people would never state the case so boldly and probably most would even deny that is what they believe. However, when you hear what some people pray for, and the way they ask for it, you realize that they are trying to force their will upon God.

But doesn't the Bible have examples of this? Aren't some situations in the Bible exactly that? Consider the example of Jesus who cursed a fig tree. On what we call Palm Sunday Jesus entered Jerusalem but then went back to Bethany to spend the night. The next morning, on Monday, he and the disciples were on their way back to Jerusalem when Jesus spotted a fig tree in full leaf. He went up to it expecting to find it as full of fruit as it was full of green leaves. He found nothing, however. Mark 11:14 says, "Then he said to the tree, 'May no one ever eat fruit from you again.' And his disciples heard him say it." The next day, Tuesday morning, Jesus and the twelve were again going to Jerusalem. They saw that the tree had withered overnight. Simon Peter said, "Rabbi, look! The fig tree you cursed has withered!"

This story causes some modern people trouble because of a misunderstanding of the concept of curse in the Bible. A curse was not what we today would call a "four-letter word." It was not "nasty" or a scatological reference. A good Oriental curse was earthy, specific, and a call to action. It might be something like these two: "May the fleas of a thousand camels infest your armpits," and "May all your teeth fall out but one, and in that one may you get a toothache." In cursing the fig tree, Jesus was calling for action on the part of his disciples and using it as an object lesson or prophetic symbolism.

This story is tied by Mark with the cleansing of the Temple. A fig tree with no fruit was exactly like a Temple which produced no fruit. The cursing of the tree was a prophetic sign. The fig tree's leaves promised fruit but there was no fruit. The tree's appearance was deceptive. It was a symbol of what Jesus had found in the Temple. It, too, looked promising. The Temple had a long history and promised seekers that they could find a place of worship, a place that would help them find God. What they found was chaos like the day after Christmas at Wal-Mart. To this farce Jesus raised his whip and his voice and said in effect, "Enough! You shall not make my Father's House a place of empty promises in which you are more interested in revenue than reverence."

You see, Jesus called for action with his curse. It was a form of prayer in that he used it to accomplish God's will. He was not simply being spiteful nor was he lashing out from hurt pride. The key is that Jesus did not try to make God do something he was unwilling to do. Jesus worked in harmony with the will of God and not against it.[1] That fact is central when we think about prayer. We pray to lay hold of God's willingness, not to make God do our will.

III. Prayer Is Not An Automatic Guarantee Of Success

A subtle misunderstanding of prayer is to think of it as a guarantee of success. Someone might think, "I really need to get an edge. I'll ask God to help me win." Now we certainly want to pray in all things but to imagine that prayer will give us a guarantee of success is immature. So how do we pray for things like our jobs and decisions we need to make? What good does prayer do in these situations? Consider the example of John Marks Templeton.

Templeton is the founder of the successful Templeton Mutual Fund Group. He is regarded as one of Wall Street's wisest investors. Many years ago he committed himself to Christ and became a man of prayer. He began to open all of the directors' and shareholders' meetings with prayer. But he points out that prayer is never used as a tool in making specific stock selections. Templeton notes, "That would be a gross misinterpretation of God's methods. What we do pray for is wisdom. We pray that the decisions we make today will be wise decisions and that our talks about different stocks will be wise talks. Of course, our discussions and decisions are

67

fallible and sometimes flawed. No one should expect that, just because he begins with prayer, every decision he makes is going to be profitable."[2] He continues, "However, I do believe that, if you pray, you will make fewer stupid mistakes."

Prayer is no substitute for hard work and personal responsibility. It helps us make decisions and work smarter but it is not an automatic guarantee of success.

IV. Prayer Is Not A Meaningless Ritual

My family has prayer at meal times. My wife and I have done this since we first married and we have taught our children to say grace at the table. This ritual is important to us and it expresses our daily gratitude for our food. Many people say a prayer at meal times, or before bed, or at a ball game. The saying of the prayers might be meaningful or it might just be a ritual performed at stated times simply because you have always done it.

We will do well to remember that such rituals can be important but they might seem strange to those who do not understand them. During the early days of our nation a traveling preacher went to a frontier town to hold religious services. The town had received very little religious influence before the preacher's arrival. He stayed with a family in town who had a little boy. On the first evening of his arrival everyone gathered around the table for supper. The preacher bowed his head and said an audible prayer. The little boy had never seen anything like that before. The child saw the preacher on the street the next day and asked, "Are you the fellow who talks to his plate?"[3]

V. Prayer Is Not A Purely Personal Religious Act With No Social Consequences

Praying is one of the most intimate things a person can do. To reach out to the God of creation with words and feelings is a tremendously personal act. In fact some people have described religion in general and prayer in particular with reference to this privacy. I have read definitions such as, "Religion is what one does with his solitude." I am not sure what that means because there are many things we can do with our solitude. Such a definition tries to paint religion and prayer as nothing more than a purely private communication between a person and God.

The problem with that definition is that it stops too soon. Prayer is personal and intimate but it is not purely private. One of the overwhelming teachings about prayer in the Bible is that prayer moves us from our selfish preoccupations to something beyond ourselves. The Book of James in the New Testament has this passage: "What good is it, my brothers, if a man claims to have faith but has no deeds? Can such faith save him? Suppose a brother or sister is without clothes and daily food. If one of you says to him, 'Go, I wish you well; keep warm and well fed,' but does nothing about his physical needs, what good is it? In the same way, faith by itself, if it is not accompanied by action, is dead" (2:14-17).

Prayer, in other words, should move us not only toward God, but toward our fellow humans. Frederick Douglass was a slave who narrated his life in a book that was first published in 1845. He told of the conditions under which he lived. Consider one section from his autobiography: "There were four slaves of us in the kitchen — my sister Eliza, my aunt Priscilla, Henry, and myself; and we were allowed less than a half a bushel of corn-meal per week, and very little else, either in the shape of meat or vegetables. It was not enough for us to subsist upon. We were therefore reduced to the wretched necessity of living at the expense of our neighbors. This we did by begging and stealing, whichever came handy in the time of need, the one being considered as legitimate as the other. A great many times have we poor creatures been nearly perishing with hunger, when food in abundance lay smouldering in the safe and smoke-house, and our pious mistress was aware of the fact; and yet that mistress and her husband would kneel every morning, and pray that God would bless them in basket and store!"[4]

How does that stack up against the instruction of James?

VI. Prayer Is Not Getting In Touch With Mystical Powers

We live in an age of generic spirituality. We often hear about spiritual values but by that term many people mean inner personal values rather than a reference to God. A term that is often associated with spirituality today is New Age. That is something of a catch-all term that lumps all religious, metaphysical, and spiritual quests into the same category. It might include channeling, Tarot cards, belief in reincarnation, and other such manifestations. I have noticed that some people use any talk of religious values to include even the major religions such as Judaism and Christianity.

So what is prayer in New Age philosophy? It is the attempt to get in touch with the mystical forces of the universe and to influence those forces. That is done through repeating a mantra — a special word or phrase — or by deeply meditating. The attempt to influence the powers of the universe traditionally has been called magic.

Magic is defined this way: "1. The art that purports to control or forecast natural events, effects, or forces by invoking the supernatural. 2. The practice of using charms, spells, or rituals to attempt to produce supernatural effects or to control events in nature."[5]

Christian prayer is different from all of this because it seeks to get in touch with, not a what, but a Whom. In other words prayer reaches out to God as a loving Heavenly Father who wants the best for his children rather than to a mysterious, capricious force of nature.

All of these things, then, tell us a little about what prayer is not. Prayer is not a lottery. It is not a twisting of God's arm to make him do what we want. Prayer is not an automatic guarantee of success. It is not a meaningless ritual. Nor is prayer merely a private act with no consequences. Prayer is not getting in touch with the mystical forces of the universe. It is communicating with God, the creator and sustainer of all life. No wonder prayer is misunderstood. But it is too important to be left to chance. Let us continue in our pilgrimage of learning how to pray.

---

1. For more on this see Don M. Aycock, *Eight Days That Changed The World* (Grand Rapids: Kregel Publications, 1997), chapter 2.

2. John Marks Templeton, *The Templeton Plan: 21 Steps to Success and Happiness*, as described by John Marks Templeton to James Ellison (San Francisco: A Giniger Book in association with Harper & Row, 1987), p. ix.

3. Ross Phares, *Bible in Pocket, Gun in Hand: The Story of Frontier Religion* (Lincoln: University of Nebraska Press, 1971 [1964]), p. 6.

4. Frederick Douglass, "Narrative of the Life of Frederick Douglass," in *The Classic Slave Narratives*, edited and introduced by Henry Louis Gates, Jr. (New York: Penguin Books USA, 1987), p. 286.X

5. *The American Heritage Dictionary of the English Language*, 1969 edition. S.v., "magic."

Taking The Long Look
Jeremiah 32

What preacher has not stood up to proclaim the word and wondered secretly, "Why am I doing this? Does it make any difference to anyone? Is there any future in this?" I have wondered if my sermon this week can really make a difference in anyone's life. At times I feel like a wren trying to build a nest in a hurricane. My best efforts seem blown away. This dilemma that all preachers face is poised on the boundary between the short-term effect of preaching and its long-term effect. This dilemma is not new, either. It is as old as humanity and was given voice in the prophet Jeremiah's time. Jeremiah, too, wondered if there was a future for which to plan.

I. Setting The Scene

In order to understand chapter 32, it must be set in its context. It describes a time in the year 588 B.C. in which Jerusalem was under siege by the Babylonian army and Jeremiah was a prisoner in the palace court. In 593 B.C. Psammetichus II assumed the throne of Egypt. He was a powerful military ruler and began to interfere in the affairs in Palestine and in Asia. This policy caused other nations to rebel, especially Judah, Tyre, and Ammon. By 589 B.C. they went into open revolt against Babylon.

The ruler of Babylon, Nebuchadnezzar, was still in control, however. In January of 588 B.C. he placed a blockade against Jerusalem. Jeremiah 34:7 tells of his strategy. Nebuchadnezzar simply took the outlying fortresses around Jerusalem and slowly tightened the noose around its neck. By that year, only Lachish and Azekah were left. By the summer of 588 B.C. the Babylonian troops were laying siege to Jerusalem.

In the midst of all this, Jeremiah counseled the people not to rebel but to submit to Babylon. This got him into trouble and people branded him as a traitor. Chapters 21 and 27 give more detail. Jeremiah prophesied that the only way King Zedekiah and Judah could survive was to surrender to Babylon. This did not make him popular with the people.

Zedekiah and the people of Judah thought that perhaps Jeremiah was right about God. Perhaps their only hope lay in obedience to God. They had a covenant renewal ceremony, which was something like a revival. Since Deuteronomy 15 specifies that Hebrews were not to have Hebrew slaves, the people in Judah released their slaves. Chapter 34:8-10 of Jeremiah spells out all of this.

These actions have been called "desperation religion" and "foxhole religion." The people were in a bad fix and would try anything to get out of it. The strategy seemed to work. The forces of Psammetichus II of Egypt arrived at Jerusalem about this same time and the Babylonians retreated. Feeling safe, the people of Jerusalem forgot about their newly made religious commitments and took back the slaves they had released (see Jeremiah 34:11-16). God's judgment was swift and sure. He said through Jeremiah that the Babylonians would return, which they soon did, and would burn the city and make Judah a desolation (see Jeremiah 34:17-22; and 37:3-10).

When the siege was lifted Jeremiah tried to leave Jerusalem in order to redeem a piece of land to which he was heir. When he tried to leave the city he was arrested and accused of treason (37:11-21). Jeremiah was put into prison, but then later released to house arrest in Zedekiah's court. There he was given food.

Under the Babylonian siege conditions in Jerusalem were pathetic. Food and water ran out. Jeremiah 19:9, Ezekiel 5:10, and Lamentations 2:12, 19-20 and 4:4, 7-10 all paint a gruesome picture. People were so desperate that they resorted to cannibalism with their children.

At times, all seems lost. Despair seems to be the password. The citizens of ancient Jerusalem knew this. The modern preacher staring out over the congregation sees hollow eyes staring back. Despair is an acid which eats away at confidence and faith. At times, all people, even Christians, might feel the downward pull of despair. But to give up and say, "What's the use?" is of little positive value. Even Jeremiah knew near-despair, but he never simply gave up. That is his legacy to modern people who love Christ and try to do as he teaches.

The end of Jeremiah 32 is a dialogue between the prophet and God. Jeremiah wondered how and why certain events happened as they did. He wondered about God's power to accomplish what he promised. The answer he received is surprising to the prophet and to modern readers. First, though, let us consider the symbolic act of faith which Jeremiah undertook ...

II. Symbolic Faith

When no food is available, of what use is property? During the siege of Jerusalem property values had plummeted. Despair was rampant and the people thought they would all die. Even silver and gold was of little value because there was nothing to buy. And land? Who would buy land when the Babylonian army was camped on it?

Yet, this is precisely what Jeremiah did. In verses 6-7 he said that the word of the Lord came to him and told him to redeem the family property in Anathoth. Anathoth was a northern suburb of Jerusalem. The property seems to have been something like the family farm. Jeremiah had the right to redeem it from creditors. We saw how he had once tried to do it but was arrested and beaten up for his trouble (37:11-15). But he heard God saying to him, "Go ahead and buy it." So Jeremiah set out once more to purchase this field.

When you consider it, this is a funny picture. Judah was in shambles and Jerusalem was a wreck because of the Babylonian siege. But Jeremiah set out to buy land on which the enemy had been camping. No wonder some of the inhabitants of Jerusalem thought he was mad! Part of the dark humor here is that perhaps his family also thought he was mad and could "dump" a worthless piece of property on Jeremiah. They offered him a deal he could not refuse.

The prophet was not in this land speculation alone, however. The idea was not even his, but was God's. God calls his followers to live in the light of his promises. That was the message to Jeremiah, and also the message to contemporary Christian preachers. What things in modern life seem to be "occupied territory"? What areas of your life seem to resemble Jeremiah's family farm with an enemy army camped on it? Each of us could name one or more situations which seemed hopeless. Christian hope indicates that out of the situations come hope and life and redemption.

Your "occupied territory" might be questionable health. It might be a family matter that no one else even suspects. It could be finances which have too much month left at the end of the paycheck. More than likely it is a position in a church which does not respect you and which questions your ability as a proclaimer of the word. So what do you do? Quit? Get into something respected like the used car market?

When Jeremiah bought his field, he was speaking of his hope for the future. His action was symbolic and it spoke of the hope he had that God would not allow the Babylonians to completely eradicate the Jews. As such, his attitude was even more patriotic than that of his countrymen. He genuinely believed in the future of his country.

In verses 13-14, Jeremiah told his scribe Baruch to place the deeds in the jar "that they may last a long time." He intentionally took a long look into the future and staked his life, his possessions, and his faith that the siege was not the end. A doctor I heard about tells his patients not to read forever into their current problems. Let the one who has ears hear!

III. Faith For The Future

To act out of our faith is not always easy. Sometimes we would like certainty and absolutes. But we fail to realize that certainty and absolutes are no longer faith. Christians are people who move through life through a living faith, for as Paul says, "We walk by faith, not by sight" (2 Corinthians 5:7). That means, among other things, that we act according to our belief in morality, fairness, holiness, and love. Those are qualities that are given lip service in modern America in general and the church in particular. But these intangibles are not always valued for their usefulness in helping people get ahead. Do we suppose that Jeremiah's situation was all that different? Did he slide through his crises without so much as blinking or worrying?

We have little historical information to go on but we can be fairly certain of one thing: Jeremiah was as troubled about his nation's plight as anyone else. The difference was that he approached life from the standpoint of faith rather than despair. During the time of hand-wringing by the leaders, Jeremiah did something that seems almost laughable — he bought land as an act of faith that his nation still had a future.

I walked into a hospital room for a visit one day and saw a large fish hook hanging on a string from the headboard. The man in the room had cancer and I could not imagine what a fish hook had to do with his treatment. I asked him about it. He explained that he had caught the biggest fish of his life on that hook. He hung it in his hospital room as a symbol of life and hope. It reminded him of his love for life and of the outdoors. That hook was a living reminder that he wanted to get well and catch more fish, and love his family, and serve his Lord. It is no good looking for fairy tale endings in life. My friend died of cancer without ever again being able to wet his hook in his favorite bayou. That is beside the point, however. He lived — and died — in faith.

Jeremiah's field was to him what the hook was to my friend — a sign of life, of hope, and a refusal to allow despair be the final word. The call of God to redeem this land and legalize it was a call for Jeremiah to live his faith. The command of God was a command to live in faith, even in the midst of a dark crisis. One commentator has noted the situation when God's word came to Jeremiah and how it is like our own world: "Now, when everything looks hopeless. When fields and farms are not worth a penny. When there seems to be no hope, because the world is crumbling about us, and the only thing worth doing seems to be to survive by any means here and now, and never mind the consequences. When our terrible, weak, blind, human failures have got us into this mess, and we can no longer stand to analyze the guilty past or to look forward to the awful future that we have determined for ourselves. When we try to shut out memory, shut out hope, and just try to stay alive."[2] That sounds like Monday morning to a preacher!

Jeremiah did not hoard food or selfishly guard his possessions. His was not a "get rich quick" attitude. He made an investment for the future, and with that simple act, lived out God's word and will. God's word still comes in such a way. When everything seems hopeless and vague on the human level, God still has a future in store for his people — even preachers!

Think about that fact, and consider some of these vignettes from your life and mine:

* When you have to bury a loved one and the future seems a dead-end road — God still has a plan for your life.
* An unwanted divorce comes and all hope for joy and security seems gone forever — God still has a plan for your life.
* The church into which you poured so much of yourself goes sour and you feel cheated and burned out — God still has a plan for your life.
* Nothing major seems to be happening in your life, and you seem to be dying bit by bit instead of growing and blossoming — God still has a plan for your life.
* You do your best to live out your Christian commitments and to be a peacemaker, but all you get seems to be hostility and crucifixion — God still has a plan for your life.

This is one of the most fundamental lessons — and one of the hardest! — for word-slingers to learn. We do all we can but sometimes must wait for God to complete his plan in our lives. Life is not a four-lane highway in which we zip along at high speed to a sure destination. It is more like climbing through a mountain range. There are up and downs, zigzags, obstructions along the path, sometimes no path at all, and sometimes an unclear destination. It is that way with you and me, and to some extent it was that way for Jesus. Jesus clearly knew where he had come from and what his ultimate destination was. But along the way he was hurt by rejection, emotionally bruised by betrayal, and physically tortured by the cross. His near last words from the cross, "My God, why...?" remind us that there are dark, uncertain times in every life. But we hear his last affirmation, too: "Father, into your hands I commit my spirit."

The point here is that the life of faith, as Jeremiah and others have lived it, is rocky at times. But the very rocks that litter the path and cause us to change our course are the same rocks that form a solid foundation. Do not end the journey too soon.

Jeremiah bought a field out of obedience to God's revealed will. He probably did not know at the time what would happen, but the prophet had pledged his life to God. Today's believers also act out of their faith and hope.

IV. God's Assurance

The working out of God's will in the life a disciple is often a long, drawn out affair. This is what Jeremiah learned by buying the field. Life is long and often tough. Such was true for Jeremiah. In verse 15 he heard the voice of God tell him that the time would come when normal activities would pick up, activities like the buying and selling of land and houses. God's simple promise here is the promise of a future for Judah. It will not be precisely as the bygone days, but it would be a future of changes and new opportunities. For Jeremiah that was a promise, but for some in Judah that sounded more like a threat. Some people do not do well with change of any sort, especially change of the scope that was to come. Even so, God meant his word as a promise and a help.

What can we learn from Jeremiah? Consider these questions and suggestions:

* List some of the gray, uncertain areas of your life right now that you do not fully understand.
* Consider ways in which God has transformed losses in your life into gains.
* Think of areas of your life which seem to be like Jeremiah's buying a field during enemy occupation.
* Remember events in which your obedience to God and promises to others stood you in good stead during a crisis or a temptation.

An older pastor friend of mine used to tell me, "Never quit on Mondays." Perhaps Jeremiah's insight could be shortened simply to, "Never quit."

1. Elizabeth Achtemeier, *Jeremiah*, Knox Preaching Guide (Atlanta: John Knox Press, 1987), p. 96

2. Ibid., p. 97.

Tempted By Good

Matthew 4:1-11

Have you ever noticed that almost every mountaintop experience in life is followed by a valley experience? You graduate from school with great expectation of making your mark in the world, but you find out that the world doesn't exactly welcome you with open arms. You get married with the full expectation that your new spouse will relieve your loneliness and solve your problems, but you find out you are still you. Life's high moments are often followed by low times — depression and bewilderment.

If we knew our Bible a little better, these experiences would not surprise us because this happened to Jesus, too. He had gone to John the Baptizer who immersed him in the Jordan River and baptized him into a way of life which was to change the world. The heavens opened and Jesus saw the form of a dove descend upon him and heard the voice of God say, "You are my son; I am well pleased in you." What a grand and high moment! But look what happened next: "Jesus, full of the Holy Spirit, returned from the Jordan and was led by the Spirit in the desert where for forty days he was tempted by the devil."

This was a fall from the emotional mountain peaks to the valley of despondency. Jesus left John and the others by the Jordan and went off by himself into the desert to hammer out in his own mind his identity. He sought solitude to find his method of being who the voice at the baptism had proclaimed him to be. How does a man act when he is God's son?

So Jesus began to fast. Fasting is doing without something normal for the sake of something more important. He did without food because he was seeking something greater than bread. The struggle lasted for forty days. The number forty in the Bible is not just a digit. It is a symbol that something important was happening. The rains fell on Noah for forty days. The nation of Israel wandered in the wilderness for forty years. Elijah stayed on the mountain with God for forty days. Luke is saying here that something important was happening with Jesus. This was the time he was finding his mission in God's eyes, and deciding on his course of action.

That's when these three temptations came to him. You might think of temptation as a gravitational field. The further you are from it the less hold it has on you, while the closer you are to it, the stronger pull it has. Jesus was in this strong field of gravitational pull. Something important was happening to him. He was in a genuine battle for his spiritual life. We sometimes wonder if his temptations were real. Yes! They were real! This was no sham battle, but a war of wits and wills about the destiny of the one God appointed as the Savior. William James, a well-known philosopher and psychologist, once thought about his life and he wrote: "If this life be not a real fight, in which something is eternally gained for the universe by success, it is no better than a game of private theatricals from which we may withdraw at will. But it feels like a real fight."

Yes, life is a fight, and Jesus was in it. He found himself being tempted — pulled — by good. That's right — good. You see, every course offered to him was not bad in itself. The tempter never suggested that he do anything overtly immoral or unscrupulous. The actions suggested were good. But that's the problem. They were good, but for Jesus, not the best. And he was searching for the best. Consider these temptations for a moment.

I. Jesus Was Tempted To Satisfy Natural Needs With Unnatural Choices

At the end of Jesus' fast he was hungry. There's an understatement for you. You will notice that the temptations come as simple suggestions. That's what temptations are — suggestions. No one can make you yield. You have to do that yourself. And what did the devil suggest? The tempter simply suggested that Jesus make some of those little rocks that looked like loaves of bread into real loaves. What could be the harm in that?

Jesus was in the desert coming to grips with the kind of Messiah he was to be. He was settling in his own mind what he needed to do and how he needed to go about his work. The concept became clearer to him as the days dragged on. He was to be a Messiah who pointed to the deeper hunger in people, a hunger beyond bread and wine, a hunger for God. And that is the point of danger in the first temptation: concentrate on the physical necessities; focus on bread; feed the people; be a welfare reformer. These are good things, important things. You have been asked to contribute money so we could do a little to help hungry people. We care about the poor, and this is right and good. Had he allowed himself to be drawn into it, Jesus could have been a marvelous provider of basic human needs. He could have given bread and drawn great crowds to himself. But Jesus came to win people, not to bribe them.

Missionaries realized long ago that they could go into a poor country and draw hoards of people by giving away rice. But what they got for their effort was "rice Christians." When the food ran out, the people disappeared. Missionaries thus go into places without a strong witness for Christ and preach the good news of salvation first.

People can be blinded by the physical aspects of life. I used to work with a fellow named Bob. He was a nice guy, powerful of body, but weak of mind. Every day after work he would stop at a liquor store and buy a case of beer. When he got home he and his wife would sit in the back yard and kill the case. That for him was life — a cool shade tree and a cool brew. He had no interest whatever in any talk about Christ and eternal life. There are millions of people just like him.

Jesus could have gone into the bread distribution business had he wanted to. It was a necessary job, and it was a temptation. But look at his answer: "It is written: 'Man does not live on bread alone.' " There is a deeper hunger in people, a hunger that a cool beer under the shade tree won't ultimately satisfy; a hunger that weekends in the Bahamas can't fill; a thirst that new cars and nice houses and great neighbors just will not quench. The issue for Jesus was this: "Who will be the ultimate focus in my life — men or God?" He chose God. And do you know what happened? By choosing God, Jesus was set free to serve men.

This temptation and Jesus' answer is not a wholesale condemnation of things. God is not against bread or houses or cars. He is against a view of life that ignores the spiritual dimension and acts as if God does not exist. "Man does not live by bread alone," but by a deep awareness that God permeates all of life and that we never get away from him. Bread is good and necessary, but it molds and sours and must be replaced. Life cannot be built on a crust or counted by the loaf. Jesus resisted this temptation, but the battle was far from over.

II. Jesus Was Tempted To Gratify Good Ends With Bad Means

The devil failed to get Jesus to give in to the temptation to make stones into bread, or in this case, make bread more important than God. But the powers of darkness are relentless so a second temptation came to Jesus. He saw in his mind's eye the kingdoms of the world. He saw Rome with its regal splendor; Egypt with its elegant might; Babylon with its beautiful riches. They could so easily belong to Jesus if he would only tip his hat to evil. This temptation was an appeal to Jesus' ambition, and that is what made it seem good. After all, did he not come to win people? Would that task not be easier if he had power and authority?

The devil knew that Jesus' goal was to draw people back to God, so the tempter tried to get Jesus to take a short-cut to that goal. That was the problem. There is nothing necessarily wrong with power and authority. Someone has to be in control. But where would that authority come from? Could a good goal — to call people to God — be accomplished by bad means? Jesus could have had all the power he wanted to accomplish his goals. But what kind of power could demand allegiance? What type of authority could make people follow? If a person with a knife at his throat were to follow God would that count?

Power corrupts and absolute power corrupts absolutely. Jesus could have been the most powerful man on earth had he chosen to do so. But he would have failed in the very thing he wanted, namely, to win the hearts of men and women. He came to win people, not to force them. Jesus would not use people for his own glorification. Don't you hate to be used by people? I don't want to be somebody's "project" or someone's "case." I want to be treated like a person with dignity and worth. I want to be accepted for who I am. I want to love God because he loves me. What kind of God would he be if he held a dagger to my throat and asked, "Now, don't you want to follow me?"

The devil wanted to give Jesus power — pure raw power — and thought he could corrupt him with it. "Force them to follow you," he hissed. And Jesus was drawn by that gravitational pull because he wanted to succeed. But look what he answered: "It is written: 'Worship the Lord your God and serve him only.' " There was power! It was the power of absolute allegiance. This was faith that is trust in God that asks for no proof. Jesus did not ask God to up the ante. He was content to use the right means for the right end, even if it meant bypassing the short-cut to success.

Years after this event, the apostle Paul looked back on Jesus' life and proclaimed something about him that would have surprised the devil. In Philippians 2:9-11 Paul said about Jesus, "Therefore God exalted him to the highest place and gave him the name that is above every name, that at the name of Jesus every knee should bow, in heaven and on earth and under the earth, and every tongue confess that Jesus Christ is Lord, to the glory of God the Father." Jesus did not have to grasp at straws or clutch for power. He had it all along. It was different from what most people would have thought, but he had it.

He was tempted to gratify an ambition, but he resisted. Even so, the devil was not ready to give up. A third temptation came.

III. Jesus Was Tempted To Exploit A Deep Relationship With A Shallow Acquaintance

This was the most subtle of the temptations. The devil even quotes Scripture in this one. "If you are the Son of God throw yourself down from here." Then he quotes from Psalm 91: "He will command his angels concerning you to guard you carefully; they will lift you up in their hands, so that you will not strike your foot against a stone." This was a temptation for Jesus to exploit his relationship with God. "Make a spectacle of yourself," the devil said. "Create a circus. Gather the crowds and leap off the 150-foot tower to the ground below. If you are truly God's son, you won't get hurt. God will come rescue you. Go ahead. You'll see. You'll impress everyone and they will follow you."

He was teasing and goading Jesus. "How will they ever know who you are? This is your chance! Go ahead. Show them." But the problem was that his basic argument was all wrong. Yes, Jesus was God's son, but no spectacular circus act would win the people. He had come to win the people with love, not trick them with stunts. The temptation was to use his status as the unique Son of God and force God into action by jumping off the temple. That is like snake handling in church today.

How did Jesus answer? "Do not put the Lord your God to the test." There would be no exploitation of his relationship to God. There would be no compromise. Rome allowed for all types of religions to flourish in its kingdom, but it fought Christianity from the beginning. Why? Because the Christians would not compromise. They would not bow to Caesar. Doesn't that say something to us?

Jesus realized that he could not try to force God to protect him because God might have had other ideas. There is more to life than safety and comfort. Now that is hard for us to realize. But Jesus came to give his life, not to protect it. His goal was not the applause of the crowds but the single-minded devotion to the will of his Father. The shadow of the cross fell across Jesus' path from his earliest days. The cross was the symbol of shame, rejection, hatred. He took that cross as his way of saying he would not compromise with evil. He calls us to carry our crosses for him, too.

"Do not put the Lord your God to the test." Do not try to force God into doing what you want rather than what he wills. This is an awesome rebuke of the powers of darkness. It still is.

Jesus went into the desert after the high moment of his baptism. He found himself being pulled in a number of directions. He was tempted to use his powers to satisfy his need. He was tempted to take short-cuts to gratify his ambition. He was tempted to use his unique status with God to exploit that relationship. Had he yielded to any of those temptations he would have been pulled off course. He would have been like the deer hound that started out chasing a buck. A fox crossed the path and the hound began trailing the fox. After a while, a rabbit crossed the path and the hound chased the rabbit. In time a mouse crossed the trail and the hound followed the mouse to its borough. He had begun trailing a buck and ended up watching a mouse hole.

Jesus would have none of that. So he won, for the time being, because verse 12 says the devil left him "until an opportune time." Remember, opportunity may knock only once, but temptation rings forever. Let us beware.

Struggling With The Truth
Ephesians 7:10-14

Aesop told this old story. A wild boar was busily whetting his tusks against a tree in the forest when a fox came by. "Why are you wasting your time in this manner?" asked the fox. "Neither a hunter nor a hound is in sight, and no danger is at hand." "True enough," replied the boar, "but when the danger does arise, I shall have something else to do than to sharpen my weapons."

He was right, wasn't he? The time to sharpen the weapon is before the trumpet sounds and you are in the thick of battle. The price of being unprepared is often very high. Think of December 7, 1941. The Japanese "Zeros" came, practically unopposed, and heavily damaged the U. S. fleet in Pearl Harbor.

In the life of faith, preparedness is a necessity, too. This is what Paul was saying in Ephesians 6. He was aware how easily people could slip into a drowsy dullness that leaves the watchtowers unguarded. He had seen it time and again. People, good people, did not keep awake in their faith and before they knew it, they were overwhelmed by some enemy. So he wrote to his friends in Ephesus and advised them to prepare themselves because sooner or later, they would be in battle and they needed to be ready.

As Aesop had observed in his story, "It is too late to whet the sword when the trumpet sounds." How do we get ready and stay alert? It is no great mystery, for we are told in verses 13 and 14: "Therefore put on the full armor of God, so that when the day of evil comes, you may be able to stand your ground, and after you have done everything, to stand. Stand firm then, with the belt of truth buckled around your waist...." "The belt of truth buckled around your waist." There is our clue to spiritual readiness. Consider with me the matter of "struggling with the truth."

I. Christians Are In Nothing Less Than A Cosmic Battle

In battle one of the first things to do is to determine who your friends are and who the enemy is. So who or what are we fighting?

Look carefully at verses 11 and 12: "Put on the full armor of God so that you can take your stand against the devil's schemes. For our struggle is not against flesh and blood, but against the rulers, against the authorities, against the spiritual forces of evil in the heavenly realms."

We are not up against flesh and blood, but against every scheme, plan, and devious technique thought up by the devil. Paul specified several aspects of these schemes. He called them "rulers," "authorities," "powers of the dark world," and "spiritual forces of evil in the heavenly realm." We are up against "spiritual terrorists," a "hit squad." Now what does all that mean?

It means that all the powers of darkness seem to concentrate upon certain goals and targets. These "powers" and "rulers" are easy enough to see take shape and take on a life of their own. You see it when *anything* in this world is raised up to the rank of God. It might be revolution, or materialism, or communism, or democracy, or apartheid, or sex, or race, or pleasure. When any of these things is made of first importance in life, chaos is soon to follow. For example, Adolf Hitler wanted to elevate the "Aryan race," and a bloodbath followed like the earth had never witnessed. The first commandment is still in force: "You shall have no other gods before me." Not the god of race or color or nationality or anything!

We are in a battle with forces strong and unrelenting. If we yield to them, they will smother us. God's antagonists are many. They include anything that breaks life apart and pulls you to pieces. These forces are the things that seek to contradict God's purpose in your life and give you confusion. They are the things that overturn the values of love and which shatter sure standards. They are everything which undermines the stability which faith in Christ gives us and leaves us teetering on the edge of disaster. Yes, these powers of darkness are strong.

II. We Are Not In This Fight Alone

"Be strong in the Lord and in his mighty power," Paul had told his friends in Ephesus. The greatest ally you and I have is God himself. He has provided us with all the resources for waging spiritual war. We move along through life doing the best we can but wondering all the while if our best is enough. A sign I saw recently puts it cleverly: "Don't look back — they might be gaining on you." We wonder what life is all about, and what our place is. But whatever else might be said, this much is clear: God is on our side.

I do not mean that God prefers those of us in this room over other people. I simply mean that God has shown himself to be an ally to the human race. He cares what happens to us, and he works to benefit us. That is why Paul could say confidently, "Be strong in the Lord and in his mighty power." We can do that because he wants us to be strong in him.

It is not the power of your enemies that counts, but the power of your allies. That is the good news here. Not only has God shown himself to be on our side, he has also provided us with all the equipment we need to fight this spiritual battle.

"Put on the full armor of God." We have armor provided by God to wage this fight! The goal is to win because victory in this realm is too important to leave to chance. We fight with God's armor on us, as he puts it, "to stand your ground, and after you have done everything, to stand." As someone said, "The soldier's ultimate purpose is to be standing at the end of the battle while his foe lies vanquished at his feet." This battle is not the dropping of an atomic bomb from six miles up. It is hand-to-hand combat! How do you get ready for this type of battle? You put on personal armor. Paul mentions several pieces here: the breastplate of righteousness; special combat shoes; the shield of faith; the helmet of salvation. I want to zero in on the first one he lists: the belt of truth.

III. "Stand Firm Then, With The Belt Of Truth Buckled Around Your Waist"

The concept of truth is our day is really taking a beating. It is almost as if many people are intentionally fleeing truth to embrace falsehood. One U. S. Representative recently said, "There is an attitude that if you can get away with it, go ahead and lie." There is evidence to support his statement, too.

 * One study accuses 47 Harvard and Emory University scientists of producing misleading papers.

*A congressional subcommittee estimates that one of every three Americans falsifies career or educational credentials to get jobs.

*Vicious "negative campaigning" in recent elections was fueled by deliberate misinformation about opponents.

A member of the Ethics Resource Center said that when commitment to truth is thrown out the window, "trust and confidence break down, you get apathy, cynicism and, ultimately, anarchy."

But such as this belongs to the works of darkness, not to you and me. We are Christians by calling and by decision. We have renounced the powers of darkness. We have refused to have our lives fueled by lies. As Paul says, we are in a battle in which we have the "belt of truth tied around the waist."

IV. But What Is Truth?

It is a question as old as the Bible. On the day of his crucifixion Jesus stood before Pilate and said, "Everyone on the side of truth listens to me." Pilate spat back, "What is truth?" Every philosophy and way of life tries in some way to answer that challenging question.

Right after the Civil War, a host of people became teachers because they thought it was an easy way of making a living. Booker T. Washington tells about one of these fellows in his autobiography, *Up From Slavery*. This man went from village to village teaching a little and receiving pay for it. In one town the people asked if he taught that the earth is round or flat. The teacher replied that he was prepared to teach that the earth was either flat or round, according to the preference of a majority of his patrons. Truth by survey!

Even in the church we wonder about this matter of truth. You cannot help but wonder if truth is to be found in the church. But think about it this way. Suppose someone came up to you and said, "I don't know what an automobile is. Could you show me one?" Now, would you take that person to a junkyard and show him the wrecked, rusting heaps? No, you would take him to a new car showroom and point out the latest shiny model. Suppose someone said, "I don't know what truth is. Could you show it to me?" You would not show him the moral wrecks and incompetent heaps. You would take him to the source. In this case, it is Christ himself.

Christ is truth — not just the way to truth, or a teacher of the truth, but he *is* truth. In the Bible the word "truth" means, "solid," "without a hollow ring." That's it. That is Christ. There is no hollow ring to his life. He is the truth. Let us go to him.

A Slice Off The Heavenly Loaf

John 6:41-51

Jesus gave himself to hungry humankind as the bread of heaven. Imagine it! He called himself the bread of life. What did he mean? Among other things, Jesus meant that a relationship with him satisfies the deepest hungers of our lives. Consider some of these hungers.

I. All Of Us Have A Hunger For Satisfaction In Relation To Others

We want to be connected to other people and to feel valued by them. Do you remember the story of shipwrecked Robinson Crusoe? Remember that even he had his man Friday.

Dale Carnegie sold millions of copies of his book, *How To Win Friends And Influence People*. People want to be loved and needed. One of our deep needs is to have satisfaction in our relationship to other people. That satisfaction is given through Christ. He puts us together as the church and makes us brothers and sisters in him. We can rejoice at our large family.

Shared life is worthwhile and illustrated by an old story about stone soup. A beggar wandered into a village once and announced to the villagers that he had a magic stone that could make the best soup they ever tasted. The people did not believe him but one person put a pot of water on the fire to test the beggar. Once the water began to warm up, the beggar dropped his stone into it. He said, "This will be delicious soup. But if someone had a few carrots to add, it would be much better." A farmer watching the event said he had some so he dropped them in. The beggar said, "This is going to be great soup! But if someone had a bit of beef and some bacon to add, it would be even better." Two villagers went home and brought back a few chunks of meat and some bacon and dropped them in. The beggar mentioned potatoes, a little salt, and some cabbage. People brought them and placed them into the pot. Before long the villagers sat down to the best pot of soup they had ever tasted.

II. Another Hunger We Have Is Significance In Relation To The World

We ask ourselves, "Does life really matter? Am I contributing anything worthwhile?" Each of us wants to feel that way. Don't you like to feel special? Perhaps as a child you were made to feel special when your parents gave you special gifts or did little things for you that you liked. God does this for us now.

In Jesus Christ, we are given a sense of significance to him and to the world. Christians are given the special task of proclaiming the gospel and helping others to realize their salvation in Christ. Can that ever be insignificant?

III. Still Another Hunger We Have Is For Security In Relation To God

We want some assurance that God knows us and cares about what happens to us. In verse 47, Jesus gave one of his clearest words about what he offered people: "Truly, truly, I say to you, he who believes has eternal life." What he has to offer is not a matter of earning but of receiving. This life Jesus spoke of does not perish as does regular food. It is sustained, not by what one eats, but by what one believes.

Jesus gives life to everyone who believes. This, in short, is the gospel story. Christ wills salvation of everyone and offers himself as the One able to give this salvation. Verses 50 and 51 indicate that as persons eat the "living bread" offered them, they are nourished in a whole new realm — the realm of eternal life.

Jesus said, "If anyone eats of this bread, he shall live forever; and the bread also which I shall give for the life of the world is my flesh" (v. 51bc). This statement is a metaphor or word-picture. Jesus was trying to communicate the truth that he, and he alone, can offer to people what they most need. In the antebellum South many slaveholders would not allow their slaves to pray or call upon the name of God. They were afraid that the slaves' prayers might be answered. But no amount of rules or legislation can halt a person's heartfelt need to reach out to God. Many slaves would go into their cabins at night and kneel over a bucket of water and press their faces right up to the brim. That was to absorb the sound as they called out to God to rescue them and to free them.

Yes, the deepest hungers of life can be satisfied in Christ. These hungers are for satisfaction related to others, our hunger for significance in relation to the world, and our hunger for security in relation to God. All are satisfied through faith in our Lord. He is genuinely the bread of life. He invites us to come now and have a slice off the heavenly loaf.

Take Jesus Completely

John 6:51-58

Christianity is not a faith for the easily offended. It is a tough-minded faith for people who want more than just a little dab of religion here and there to round out their lives. Christianity is an all-or-nothing commitment. We are committed to Christ and his work, or we are not. One thing is certain — we cannot have it both ways.

This fact is shown nowhere more clearly than in our text for today. Jesus had earlier identified himself with the bread of heaven. He said in verse 51 that if anyone would eat of his flesh that person would live forever. Now that statement upset the Jews to no end. The good and pious Jews had strict dietary laws. We all know, for example, that they would eat no pork.

One thing certainly not on their list of approved foods was human flesh! Listen again to verse 52: "Then the Jews began to argue sharply among themselves, 'How can this man give us his flesh to eat?' " They were highly offended and repulsed by the very idea of eating human flesh. Who wouldn't be? This statement seems almost grotesque until we realize what Jesus was trying to communicate.

As was often the case, Jesus and his hearers were not on the same wave length. He was speaking to them in figurative or para-bolic language but they heard only literally. He often used stories, images, and word pictures to get his point across. That is what he was doing on the day many of his hearers felt offended. They thought Jesus had really gone off the deep end!

But are we any better off after being familiar with his words for twenty centuries? Let us ask ourselves, "What does Jesus mean when he tells us to eat his flesh and drink his blood?"

He means that we are to trust him for our spiritual nutrition. Some foods and vitamins advertise themselves with the words, "Provides 100 percent of the recommended daily allowance." That is supposed to convince us these products are good for us. What provides us all the spiritual nutrition we need? A super vitamin? A special book? How about a set of spiritual disciplines?

Jesus said that anyone who took him wholly would find his spiritual nutrition in him. When we give our lives to Christ we are given energy and health back. That is one meaning of what it means to eat his flesh and drink his blood. Jesus is the trustworthy guide and Lord of life. You and I can safely give ourselves to him and allow him to live inside us. This is mysterious but also very liberating.

To eat Jesus' flesh means to absorb him into our lives. To eat and drink is to take food inside ourselves and to allow the natural digestive processes to absorb the nutrients in the food. It becomes part of us. Jesus wants that to happen between you and him.

Christianity is all or nothing. We are totally given to Christ or we are not given at all. Jesus challenges us to absorb him into our lives so that every aspect of our lives will be changed and challenged by his presence.

If I were to ingest a small amount of arsenic every aspect of my life would change. I would be totally dead! Taking Christ into our lives has the opposite effect. We would become more alive, more responsive, more alert. He would change everything about us and that is what he wants to do.

To eat Jesus' flesh means that we accept the eternal life God offers us. The words eternal life in the Bible mean two things at the same time. We usually think of eternal life as unending life — life that goes on and on forever. That certainly is part of it. But eternal life is more than life with God forever. It is also the quality of life we experience here and now where we align ourselves with Christ. Eternal life can be had as a quality of existence today for all who open themselves to God.

"He who eats my flesh and drinks my blood has eternal life, and I will raise him up on the last day." That really is a powerful statement. It challenges and confronts us. Faith is serious business. Christ has invited us to a banquet. He himself is the meal.

Let no one go home empty.

Living The Servant Attitude

Luke 17:1-10

Jesus was a master at knowing the heart of mankind. He realized that the attitudes of the heart affected action. In this passage, he sketched out attitudes which should characterize a servant who wants to follow Christ.

I. There Is The Attitude Of Positive Leadership

Jesus spoke to his disciples and pointed out that they would find stumbling blocks to their faith everywhere. Because of this, they must be very careful how they lived, and especially how they affected others. A servant of Christ is not at liberty to do as he pleases or to disregard the feelings of others. Paul, for example, once said that if eating meat which had been sacrificed to idols caused others to stumble, then he would eat no meat. He tried to do what Jesus called for — to be a positive example in his leadership so no one would stumble and fall because of his example. This teaching points out the importance of modern disciples to live responsibly in order to help and not hurt others.

II. There Is The Attitude Of Complete Forgiveness

The servant of Christ is not simply passive in his living. He is also active. We do not only take care not to hurt others, but we also actively help them. Jesus said that if a brother sins, rebuke him. This is not an invitation to be "busy bodies." It is a command to be active in helping fellow Christians avoid the downward spiral of sin. How many church squabbles or splits could be avoided if people learned to say, "I'm sorry, please forgive me," and "Yes, I will." The church needs people who will give in to a higher good — the good of Christ and his work.

III. There Is The Attitude Of Active Faith

Who would want to plant a mulberry tree in the sea? That is hardly the question, is it? Jesus indicated that a servant with just a

101

little faith can accomplish great feats. The mulberry tree has especially deep roots. The disciples knew that Jesus meant that even difficult feats could be accomplished by active faith. One commentator said, "Faith is something which, if it exists at all in the true sense, will make any moral duty possible." Think of one or two situations in your life right now that call for an active faith. It might be a work slow down, or a health breakdown. How will you meet the challenge? Kicking and screaming, or with the kind of faith that moves impossibly deep situations and transforms every situation?

Biologists who know about fish speak of the auto-catalytic principle. This is an observation that a fish grows to the size supportable by the amount of nutritive value of the water in its habitat. In other words, a goldfish in a small bowl will remain small. Take that same fish and put it into a large pond and it will grow into a large carp. The environment makes the difference. The same is true for humans, too. Jesus invited his followers to allow their faith to enlarge their spiritual environments. Grow. Expand. Do something unusual.

IV. There Is The Attitude Of Steady Faithfulness

Verses 7 through 10 picture an ancient scene. A master has servants who worked in the fields all day. Toward evening they come back to the house and prepared a meal for the master. Jesus asked, "Which of you will say (to the servants) 'Come immediately and sit down to eat'?" No one would, of course. The master does not serve the slave, but the other way around! What is this story about?

Jesus was saying to his disciples that they are forever in God's debt. He is never in theirs. Their work is only right and proper. Jesus pointed out that the Christian can never repay the debt to God. As someone said of this story, "It is a warning against the bookkeeping mentality which thinks that it can run up a credit balance with God." The servant of God is the one who works for his Lord's goals. He or she keeps on working and asks for no thanks, pats on the back, or indebtedness on God's part.

The servant thus has these four attitudes: a steady faithfulness that keeps on working; an active faith that accomplishes good; complete forgiveness to those who might cause hurt; and a positive leadership that causes no one injury. Won't you live this servant attitude?

Fatal Mistakes

Luke 16:19-31

"But I meant well!" This defense was given by a convicted forger as he explained that he was forging checks in order to feed his hungry children. The jury was sympathetic, but not swayed in his favor. Do good intentions count? Yes, but not always. Some mistakes are minor and insignificant. Others are fatal and tragic. Let Jesus, through Luke's Gospel, tell a story which pictures a well-meaning man who made some fatal mistakes.

The background of this story is that Jesus was talking with some Pharisees "who were lovers of money," as verse 14 says. They wanted to justify themselves before others for their niggardly attitudes. Jesus then told the story we know as "The Rich Man and Lazarus." In this story Jesus pointed out some serious errors the rich man had made in attitude and action.

I. He Mistook Today For Eternity

The rich man, called Dives in the Authorized Version, is pictured as having the best of everything — regal clothes, scrumptious meals, spacious house. He had it all. No one on *The Lifestyles of the Rich and Famous* ever fared better. The trouble with this is that the rich man began to think of this life as all there is. The fine clothes and great meals blinded him to the fact that this life is not the end, but that eternity awaits all.

This mistake is still very much with us today. How often do people say or live as if, echoing an old beer commercial, "You go around only once." Dives mistook today for eternity, thinking that he would always do well. He forgot that judgment will come and that God is not impressed by fancy clothes or banquet spreads. God will ask for an accounting of life.

II. Next, He Mistook Opportunity For Privilege

The rich man had enormous opportunity to ease the suffering of the poor, especially of Lazarus who sat at his gate. This could have been done so easily as hardly to bother Dives at all. But he failed! He saw wealth as privilege rather than as an opportunity to help others.

We do not have to be rich in order to help. Contributions to food banks, clothes closets, and community chests help. Most important, though, is your getting personally involved with people in need.

III. He Mistook A Neighbor For A Nobody

The contrast between the rich man and Lazarus is striking. One had everything — food, clothing, friends to share the banquet. The other had nothing except a seat on the ground by the other's door. Lazarus had only the companion of dogs who licked his sores as a way to heal them, as they licked themselves. They cared, but the man who could have done most did not.

Dives mistook his neighbor Lazarus for a nobody. He did not speak to him, comfort him, give him anything except crumbs. In that day before napkins, people would use chunks of bread to wipe their hand on after a meal. These crumbly chunks were then thrown out. This is what Lazarus longed for. Even garbage was better than what he had. The rich man could have done so much so easily, but he did nothing. For him, Lazarus was simply a nobody.

For Dives, none of the suffering or hardship of others made any difference to him. His mind was closed to the revelation of God, and his heart was closed to the revelation of the demands of compassion. Even after death he still wanted Lazarus to be his lackey, his "boy." He told Abraham, "Send Lazarus to get me some water." He thought he was still in charge! In all of this Dives never thought of Lazarus as a real human being like himself, with a name and a history and a future. He seemed like a nameless nobody. But he did have a name. Lazarus is from the Hebrew *Eleazar* which means "God is his help." And so he was. Earthly values were reversed later and the nobody became somebody. God noticed the one whom the rich man ignored.

IV. He Mistook His Possessions For His Soul

Can't you just see Dives taking care of his expensive clothes? No treatment was too good for them — special cleaning and pressing and storage. And his other things? He built a special garage just for his Rolls Royce. He sent his servants into the market every day so they could buy only the freshest food for the meals. They cleaned the mansion daily and made sure it was spotless.

The rich man neglected one thing, however — his soul. He had made the fatal mistake of thinking that his things fully comprised his life. He was probably a Sadducee and believed in no afterlife, although he had the law and the prophets. Amidst all of the elaborate preparation and care he took, Dives neglected the thing of greatest value — his very self. Was he not like the one about whom Jesus spoke as he told the story of a farmer who built bigger barns? On the night of the completion of the building expansion God said to him, "You fool, this night your soul will be required of you."

Dives made some fatal mistakes in his relationships with other people, with God, and even with himself. You do not want to make the same mistakes, do you?

Accepting And Rejecting Jesus
John 6:67

One of the strangest aspects of faith is that people can go away from faith as well as come to it. I say this is strange because most of us seldom think about people rejecting their faith and going away. We usually think of people coming to Christ, accepting baptism or some other sign of confirmation, and then living in close harmony with the Lord the rest of their lives. That often does happen. Sometimes, though, people are like those in our text. They turn their backs on Christ and desert him.

Some modern Christians have a dreamy notion that life in New Testament times was categorically different from life today. One person said to me, "If I had just lived in Jesus' time, I might have met him in person. Surely I would have believed!" Perhaps that is true, but it might not be. Not everyone who met Jesus followed him. Not everyone who heard him teach decided to believe.

Verses 66 and 67 make clear the fact that Jesus' teaching about eating his flesh and drinking his blood were just too much for some. Verse 66 says, "As a result of this many of his disciples withdrew, and were not walking with him anymore." The word "disciples" here does not refer to the twelve disciples whom Jesus chose, but to people who had followed Jesus while he was giving away bread. Large crowds came to him, but when Jesus told them truths they were unwilling to hear, they turned away from him.

The entire sixth chapter of John is essential for understanding the conflict and rejection of these people. They wanted to make Jesus their king but it had to be on their terms. Jesus refused. They were willing to follow him if he would be the kind of Messiah they wanted. He turned the tables and demanded they accept him on his term, not their own. When that happened, many of them rejected him.

The situation is not greatly different today. People are still trying to squeeze Jesus into their own mental molds. They try to make him over into their image rather than allow him to make them in his image. Do some of your friends do this? Today's text is a good corrective to our temptation to make Jesus fit our wishes.

When the superficial disciples fled, Jesus asked the twelve, "You do not want to go away also, do you?" What a poignant question! Look at who is left. Someone pointed out that chapter six opens with 5,000 excited warriors (v. 15) and closes with twelve troubled disciples, one of whom was a traitor!

Why do people reject him? There are many reasons. Some people have never known the real Christ. They might have heard something about him from a friend or on a televised worship program. But these impressions might be misleading and may fail to bring a person to the living Christ. Another reason why people reject Jesus is because of the actions and attitudes of some of Christ's people. Others look at us and say, "If that is what a Christian is, I want no part of it."

Still others try to follow Christ for a while but soon tire out on the journey. They simply quit. They might be severely disappointed with what they got compared to what they were promised. Others lived vile and degraded lives and want nothing to do with the moral demands of the gospel.

Jesus' question to his disciples is poignant: "You do not want to leave, too, do you?" This question by Jesus expressed his disappointment with the shallow followers. He came into this world to save sinners. His offer of eternal life was rejected by many and Jesus was clearly disappointed. He still is. People who hear his message and turn him away hurt not only themselves, but also hurt Christ. In his own time, not everyone rejected him, however.

Some rejected Jesus, but not everyone did. In verses 68 and 69, Simon Peter answered the question posed by Jesus in the previous verse. He wanted to know if they were going to leave him also. Simon's answer is a classic: "Lord, to whom shall we go? You have words of eternal life. And we have believed and have come to know that you are the Holy One of God." This statement was a recognition that the longing for eternal life, humankind's deepest hunger, is satisfied only in Christ.

What exactly does the New Testament mean by the term "eternal life"? It has been defined as "the never-ending experience of living with God." It begins with a person's conversion and continues for eternity. Thus, it has quantity. Eternal life also has quality. It is the inner life of a person who has said "Yes" to Christ. Such a person becomes more and more like the person God intends for him or her to become. Eternal life is a quality of life on earth which leads to quantity of life in heaven.

Jesus' disciples knew they had nowhere else to go. Really now, do we today? There are plenty of substitutes and false gods, but only one Lord. Jesus is the Bread of Life which satisfies our deepest hungers for significance and relationships.

Christ comes to us with an offer. The offer is for us to accept him as our Lord and savior. He forces no one to do so and asks only for commitment to him. What will you do with this offer?

Will you reject or accept Jesus Christ?

Riches Are More Than Money

Mark 12:41-44

Someone has suggested that the way you can tell something about another person is by examining the stubs of this person's checkbook. In this way you can determine what she values, and what he is willing to spend hard cash on. Mark pictures this vignette from the life of Jesus in which he was examining the stubs from the checkbooks of his contemporaries.

He was sitting in the Temple area where the offerings were put. Isn't that curious? He just sat there and watched for a while. A vast array of people came by. The Scribes seemed to march in and with great fanfare they dropped in their offerings with the "clink" of the gold against the coffers. The Pharisees strutted in and with all eyes trained upon them spread their silver against the offering box. The splash of colors and the noise of the metal had created quite a show for Jesus.

But then an old woman shuffled in. She did not want any notice and probably would have been embarrassed had she known Jesus was watching. She had no gold or sliver to ring the coffers, no jewels to dazzle the eyes of observers. All she had was two small copper coins similar to our pennies. She literally put her two cents' worth in!

Jesus watched this and saw her willingness to give everything she owned to the work of God. And that caught his attention. He called his disciples to himself and said that the widow had actually put more into the treasury than had all the others. Why? The others had given from abundance while the widow had contributed from her poverty. Jesus suggested that the widow was actually the rich one there. You see, there is far more to riches than money.

I. God Counts Us Rich When We Give Out Of Our Love

In ancient Jewish society, widows was excused from giving anything to the Temple treasury. These women were considered extremely poor because there were no social benefits for them.

She could have forgotten about the Temple and its needs, but she did not. This woman contributed out of her love for God. She gave out of a sense of love, and not because of the pressure of others.

This is one reason why Jesus suggested she was rich. Although she was a widow, she had not lost her love and concern for God and for people. This ancient widow did not worry about what she did *not* have. She did not spend her time bemoaning her situation. Instead, she showed us something vital for healthy living, namely, use what you have in love. Whatever it might be, it is enough.

II. God Counts Us Rich When Our Giving Costs Us Something

A ten-dollar donation to the church from a millionaire costs this person nothing. The absence of the money is not even noticed. But a ten-dollar donation by a person on Social Security drawing 225 dollars a month is costly. This is what Jesus noticed about the widow and the rich people in the Temple. Most gave out of their wealth, and Jesus did not condemn them. But they had plenty and did not even miss the money. But the widow gave something that cost her. She missed it, and thus it was worth something.

A devout woman living in Kentucky was married to a man who had no use for the church. She felt that she should contribute to her church but her husband would not give her the money to do so. She came upon the idea of saving money in her shopping by using coupons. Her husband would give her an allotment for the week's groceries. Whatever she could save off the grocery bill she would give to her church. This sometimes amounted to only a few quarters per week. Her offering cost her a great deal, but it proved her rich toward God.

III. God Counts Us Rich When We Give In Faith

The widow in Mark's story felt no coercion from the people. They put no pressure on her to contribute to the Temple. Further, she made no complaints about her lot in life. Yet she was heartily commended by Jesus because of her faith in giving. You see, she gave what she had in faith because she literally gave away her last dime. Here was a woman who did not know where her next meal might come from, but that did not stop her.

Faith in God includes faith in the future. The widow knew that whatever might come, God could be trusted to take care of her. This faith made her very rich toward God. You and I are thus called to such a faith.

We can be rich toward God when we give out of love. We can have more than we imagined when our giving costs us something personally. And we are rich in faith when our actions, including our giving, come from faith.

Riches, you see, are far more than money.

Toward An Active Faith
Mark 4:35-41

Faith is active and alive. Faith is never just some fuzzy belief about something opaque and indefinite. It has muscle and backbone, and it breathes with the ability to do what it sets out to do.

No one knew this better than Jesus. He lived such a short life, yet he accomplished so very much. Consider the incident we have read about today. He asked his disciples to put out into the lake in a small fishing boat. Jesus had been teaching the crowds and was drained and sleepy, so as the others rowed, he stretched out for a little nap. As he slept a quick storm brewed up on the lake. That set the stage for a great teaching event. The disciples got scared during the storm so they woke Jesus up. Can you imagine that? He was sleeping through a storm!

That in itself was part of what his disciples learned, at least later. There are times to work, but there are times to sit back and not worry so much. It is like a man who once applied for a job on a farm. The farmer asked him what his qualifications were, and the man said, "Well, I can sleep through a storm." The farmer thought that was a strange answer, but he needed a hand, so he hired him. One night a couple of weeks later the farmer woke up and heard the rain pouring down and the wind howling. He got up and went to check on the farm. He found that the barn was closed up tightly and the animals were safe. All the equipment was in the shed where it belonged, and in general, everything was in good shape. It was then that it dawned on the farmer what his hand had meant when he told him he could sleep through a storm. He did his work when he was supposed to do it, and he did it well, and did not need to worry if a storm blew up in the middle of the night.

It was this kind of thing that let Jesus sleep in the boat. But the disciples were not nearly as sure of themselves as he was, so they interrupted the nap and asked this biting question: "Lord, don't you even care if we drown?" As we look back on the story we can tell the answer to that question, but for those men in the boat it was a life or death situation! Jesus' response stilled the storm immediately. "Quiet! Be still!" he said. That literally means, "Be muzzled." Then he turned the question back on the others in the boat: "Why are you so afraid? Do you still have no faith? "

What did he mean? Was he asking if they believed in him? Yes, it was that, but it was more than that, too. Jesus wanted to know if their faith was a verb, if it was active and alive. He wanted to know if it was something that would lead to action. Action under pressure can be an act of faith, too.

Jesus is still asking that question of his believers. "Do you believe to the point of acting on your belief?" That is a tough question! What makes it so hard is that so many things seem to get in the way of our belief. We are pulled from every side by someone or something vying for our attention and our time. Our faith is challenged by so many storms, and so many events which seem to remove our will to follow Christ.

We are tempted to blind ourselves to what we know is true. Jesus gives us sight in our faith, and people come along and say things to us like, "Oh, come on now, you don't really believe all that religious stuff, do you?" Or we run into a moral situation in which we know what the right thing is, but we are tempted to look the other way, or to act in a non-Christian way. The choice is often between blinding ourselves or summoning our courage and doing what is right. Across twenty centuries we hear that ancient question echo in our consciences: "Why are you so afraid? Do you still have no faith?"

When we put faith into action changes start to occur, both in our own lives and the lives of others. Think of that. Things can be different! This story of Jesus and his disciples reminds us that faith helps us to do some things that other people do not do. It has always been this way. Wherever the people of God have obeyed him they have been called on to do what seemed strange to others. Think of the strange plan of a campaign recorded in the book of Joshua, chapter 6. The Israelite army was told to march around the city of Jericho six times, and then blow the horns. They were told that the walls would then fall down and they could go in and win their battle. Can't you just see them when they first heard these instructions? They probably looked at each other and said, "This is a strange command." But they did it, and the walls of Jericho fell.

God has always required faith from his people. And faith is a verb. It is action and not just passive belief. What happens to you when you find yourself in one of life's storms? Can you believe that you are not in it alone? And believing it, can you conduct yourself in such a way as to live out your faith?

An old parable tells about a trickster who broke into a store one night. He did not steal anything, but just went around the store rearranging the price tags. The shoppers were shocked the next morning when they found diamonds selling for a few dollars, and costume jewelry priced at thousands.

In a sense, the gospel is like that. It reprices everything. It shows that some of what others consider to be of great value is practically worthless. It also shows that much of what some consider of no value is really a priceless treasure. Your faith is that priceless treasure. It is alive and active. The question is really not only "What do you believe?" but also "What do you live?"

Jesus once took a boat ride with his disciples. At the end of the journey they were not quite the same. They witnessed something rather incredible. Life took on new meaning because of that day. The gospel is wide open for you to believe, and especially for you to live. You will never quite be the same!

Searching For Jesus
John 6:24-35

Some people say that our generation is becoming godless. But make no mistake about it. Many people are looking for Jesus. They would love him as we do if they knew where and how to find him. That is the problem. They do not know where Christ is and how to reach out to him. Some searches take people to unexpected places and give surprising results.

For example, Columbus searched for a new route to Asia and found America instead. Louis Pasteur tried to find a way to keep wine from souring and came up with the pasteurization process instead. Alexander Graham Bell wanted to improve the telegraph but wound up with the telephone. Roentgen worked to find a better light for photography but invented the X-ray instead. Sometimes we do not find what we are searching for.

In today's text the people had been with Jesus and were fed. But the Lord had many other people to feed so he and the disciples left and went to the far side of the Sea of Galilee. When the people realized that Jesus and the others were gone, they got into their own boats and crossed over to Capernaum to find Jesus. Why? They wanted more bread. Some people search for Jesus through physical means.

This clamoring for bread is certainly real today, too. Hunger is all around us and hungry people need to be fed. Jesus himself commanded that. However, he was aware that people can get so preoccupied with physical needs (and wants) that they are in danger of missing their deepest need — the need for eternal life.

Jesus was not asking people to quit their jobs and never be concerned about their next meal. His point was that people should attend to matters of enduring significance. All else perishes. Even the finest of meals lasts only a day and then the person must eat again. Someone has noted, "Regardless of a person's religious presuppositions, he eventually discovers that anything tangible —

whether food or drink or sex or possessions — furnishes only transient fulfillment. This sense of incompleteness which every man experiences as a result of his efforts to find satisfaction in earthly things provides the basis on which he may be prompted to search for heavenly things that bring lasting satisfaction to life."[1]

Jesus does not condemn bread. He simply invites people to move beyond the earthly and the physical to a relationship with him. This is what Christian pilgrimage is all about.

The crowd in Capernaum also wanted a miracle. Verse 30 indicates that the people wanted a miracle. They had been given free bread once and wanted it again. They asked Jesus, "What miraculous sign then will you give that we may see it and believe you?" This is the way some today search for Jesus. They seem to need a big production, a magnificent show, a miracle every hour to confirm their pilgrimage. But is that how God intends it?

Miracles in the Bible are there for the purpose of showing that God could and did act among his people. Jesus fed the five thousand to demonstrate his Lordship and invite them to faith. His word to us today is that we need not be clamoring for miracles and a big show.

How do we find Jesus? He tells us himself in verse 35. He said that he is the bread of life and that anyone who would come to him would never go away hungry. Some search for him through physical means and others through elaborate miracles. Jesus said we would find him through faith. Yes, that is it. Faith. It is a simple as that.

Only Christ can satisfy the longing people have for eternal life. That is the long and the short of the gospel story. Have you ever been outside on a clear night and found yourself looking up at the stars? Perhaps you wanted a relationship with Whomever might be up there. That longing might have been so strong you could taste it. That is the sort of hunger the Bread of Life satisfies.

What do you value most in life? It is a difficult question for most people to answer. But we need to be realistic about it. If our desires and dreams are for this world only, then that is all we get. If we are hungry for heaven, however, through faith in Christ we get it. During this week, perhaps you can spend some time probing and exploring your deepest values. If you are hungry for a relationship with God, then pull up a chair at the his table and dine on the Bread of Life. You really are invited to this meal.

---

1. William Hull, "John," *The Broadman Bible Commentary,* Volume 9 (Nashville: Broadman Press, 1970), p. 273.

Dealing With Disappointment

Mark 4:26-34

How do you deal with disappointment? Some of us get angry. Others take the old "sour grapes" attitude — "Oh, I didn't really want that anyway." Still others try even harder to get what they were originally after. Sooner or later, we all come to grips with disappointments in our lives.

Jesus told the parable in today's text to a group of disciples who were impatient with the slow results of their work. Even though they were new at what they were doing, still they wanted action, and they wanted it immediately! Jesus' parable is a reminder that God's kingdom was not in their hands. It was in God's control. The seed germinates and grows silently in the dark, damp soil. A tiny mustard seeds grows up to become a huge plant. The growth of God's rule on earth follows that pattern. Jesus' disciples came to some realizations which help us.

First, all genuine progress is slow. This is true for civilization as a whole and for our lives in particular. You are the person you have been becoming all your life. You did not arrive at this time and place instantly. Neither your virtues nor your vices were formed overnight.

In Jesus' time, some of his disciples were impatient. One group in his day was called the Zealots. They were impatient with God so they tried to force his hand and make him usher in the Kingdom according to their schedule. Some scholars think that Judas Iscariot may have been a Zealot. He died disappointed that his idea of a kingdom never came into being.

When we find ourselves disappointed, remember that some things cannot be changed. For example, time cannot be pushed. A slow but certain rhythm is built into the universe, and we cannot change it. What we do is learn to live within the constraints of change and progress. This is not a call for complacency or apathy. It is instead a biblically realistic call to realize that some things simply take time. The seed grows quietly and unnoticed.

Next, remember that God is in control and works at his own pace. Paul said in Philippians 1:6: "And so I am sure that God, who began this good work in you, will carry it on until it is finished on the Day of Christ Jesus." This is true on both a personal and global level.

These parables about the seeds, especially the mustard seed, proclaim that mighty forces come from small beginnings. God's kingdom, his Lordship, is spreading and cannot be stopped. Even when things look dark and it seems as if the forces of evil and chaos are winning, we must remember that the seed of the Kingdom is growing.

In London during the Second World War a church was decorated to celebrate harvest homecoming. The blitz began and the building was destroyed before the celebration could begin. Some of the sheaves of corn were scattered by the bombs. During the next spring, a small patch of corn began to grow through the rubble of the church. Life will not be stifled.

Jesus pictured a tiny mustard seed sprouting and growing into a plant big enough for birds to nest. That seed he spoke of is faith. Faith keeps people going when they seem to have reached their end. Alexander Solzhenitsyn spent time in a Soviet prison camp. He tells of his experience in the novel, *One Day In The Life of Ivan Denisovich*. In a bitterly cold work camp in Siberia only one thing kept him, and others, going. That one thing was faith.

Hear the gospel in these parables. God is alive and active. His kingdom is growing like a seed germinating in the soil. From tiny origins come great results. We may aid the sowing and the reaping, but the seed is up to God.

People sometimes get disappointed with the church and with God. They ask, "Why don't we do more? Why doesn't he do more?" Jesus gave a partial answer when he said that God's kingdom moves in ways we may not even perceive.

Don't give up!